# simple chess

## mastering the basic principles

by John Emms

Everyman Publishers plc   www.everyman.uk.com

First published in 2001 by Everyman Publishers plc, formerly Cadogan Books plc, Gloucester Mansions, 140A Shaftesbury Avenue, London WC2H 8HD

Reprinted 2002.

**British Library Cataloguing-in-Publication Data**
A catalogue record for this book is available from the British Library.

ISBN 1 85744 238 5

Distributed in North America by The Globe Pequot Press, P.O Box 480, 246 Goose Lane, Guilford, CT 06437-0480.

All other sales enquiries should be directed to Everyman Chess, Gloucester Mansions, 140A Shaftesbury Avenue, London WC2H 8HD
tel: 020 7539 7600  fax: 020 7379 4060
email: dan@everyman.uk.com
website: www.everyman.uk.com

EVERYMAN CHESS SERIES (formerly Cadogan Chess)
Chief advisor: Garry Kasparov
Commissioning editor: Byron Jacobs

Typeset and edited by First Rank Publishing, Brighton.
Production by Book Production Services.
Printed and bound in Great Britain by The Cromwell Press Ltd., Trowbridge, Wiltshire.

# CONTENTS

# BIBLIOGRAPHY

**Books**
*Bishop v Knight: the verdict*, Steve Mayer (Batsford 1997)
*Dynamic Chess Strategy*, Mihai Suba (Pergamon 1991)
*Easy Guide to the Nimzo-Indian*, John Emms (Everyman 1998)
*Encyclopaedia of Chess Openings volumes A-E* (Sahovski Informator 2001)
*Endgame Secrets*, Christopher Lutz (Batsford 1999)
*Judgement and Planning in Chess*, Max Euwe (Batsford 1998)
*Kramnik: My Life and Games*, Vladimir Kramnik and Iakov Damsky (Everyman 2000)
*My System, 21st Century Edition*, Aron Nimzowitsch (Hays 1991)
*Positional Play*, Mark Dvoretsky and Artur Yusupov (Batsford 1996)
*Positional Sacrifices*, Neil McDonald (Cadogan 1994)
*Queen's Gambit Declined*, Matthew Sadler (Everyman 2000)
*Secrets of Modern Chess Strategy*, John Watson (Gambit 1998)
*Simple Chess*, Michael Stean (Faber & Faber 1978)
*The Development of Chess Style*, Max Euwe and John Nunn (Batsford 1997)
*The Games of Robert Fischer*, Robert Wade, Kevin O'Connell et al (Batsford 1972)
*The Mammoth Book of the World's Greatest Chess Games*, Graham Burgess, John Nunn and John Emms (Robinson 1998)
*The Oxford Companion to Chess*, David Hooper and Kenneth Whyld (Oxford 1996)
*Understanding Chess Move by Move*, John Nunn (Gambit 2001)
*Understanding Pawn Play in Chess*, Dražen Marović (Gambit 2000)
*Winning Pawn Structures*, Alexander Baburin (Batsford 1998)
*Winning with the Philidor*, Tony Kosten (Batsford 1992)

**Periodicals**
*ChessBase Magazine*
*ChessPublishing.com*
*Informator*
*The Week in Chess*

# INTRODUCTION

In the beginning, I, like many others, found chess to be a simple game. Just move your pawn to e4, bishop to c4, queen to h5, capture on f7 and hey presto, it's checkmate! I lost count of the number of games I won in that manner at infant's school.

Okay, so this could only last so long. Gradually my opponents wised up and I realised that a more refined approach was required for continued success. By this time, however, I was already geared up with a warehouse full of tactical tricks to spring on my unsuspecting victims. Winning material was the aim of the game and mine were full of forks, pins and skewers. Once up on material, the rest of the game was an easy 'hoovering up', promoting pawns and checkmating operation.

But even this couldn't last. Suddenly my next plateau was reached – my more experienced opponents wouldn't fall for any of my tricks anymore. Worse than this, they were slowly but surely grinding me down to defeat with something called 'positional chess'. Finally the real work had to begin.

This book is aimed as an introduction to positional chess; what to do when you reach a level where the phrase 'chess is 99% tactics' is no longer applicable; what to think about when your opponents see your traps even before you've set them; how to exploit a minute advantage such as a better pawn structure or an opponent's badly placed piece.

Part of the inspiration for this book originally stemmed from when I moved to Kent and began getting involved more and more with chess coaching at junior levels. A few years ago I came across Michael Stean's original *Simple Chess* and was so impressed with the style and clarity of his work that I began using many of his examples when coaching. I discovered that these examples successfully managed to get the important points across to the young players, and this led to an improvement of their understanding and practical play.

I do have a confession to make, however. It was only recently that I finally got round to reading Nimzowitsch's *My*

*System.* So I guess it is possible to become a grandmaster without reading the classics! However, perhaps my journey wouldn't have taken so long if I had taken the time to read it fifteen years ago.

At least I now feel in more of a position to add some of my own thoughts on positional chess, trying to reflect some of the slight changes in modern chess strategy, and studying more up-to-date battles between the grandmasters of today. As I've said before, this book is in the main an introduction to many of the important positional aspects of the game. In some topics I delved further than in others, but I hope this is down to practical usefulness as well as my own interest in the subject.

I decided to split the book into three sections: pieces, pawns and other positional ideas. The first three chapters deal with how to and how *not* to take care of your pieces. This includes aspects such as how to use 'good' and 'bad' bishops, how to create, exploit and fight for outposts, and how to use open files and diagonals.

Chapters 4-6 deal with pawns and the different structures commonly found in practice. This includes doubled pawns, isolated pawns, backward pawns, hanging pawns, pawn majorities and pawn minorities. Also in this section I deal with the Isolated Queen's Pawn (IQP), something which has always interested me and occurs surprisingly often in practice.

Finally we deal with further positional aspects such as space, colour complexes, prophylaxis, opposite coloured bishops and positional sacrifices.

Naturally there will be some overlap. Many of the examples studied contain more than one positional characteristic. For example, where there's a backward pawn, you're more than likely to find an outpost and, possibly, a 'bad' bishop. It's very rare to find a modern game to have only one positional feature, although many have one *dominant* positional feature.

I make no apologies for the fact that many samples of my own games have crept in. For one thing it's easier for me to remember my thoughts during the game and much of this is, as yet, unpublished. Also, from both my own experience of annotating other people's games and seeing the results of people annotating my games, I know how much more difficult it is to annotate when you are personally not involved. It's easy to miss a critical moment and no amount of study can make up for not having the experience of living through both the game and the post-mortem.

Finally I would like to thank Chris Ward for some material and my editor Byron Jacobs for his patience and support.

John Emms,
Kent, October 2001

# CHAPTER ONE

## Outposts

In this first section of the book we will be concentrating on pieces more than pawns, but as you will see, it's very difficult to study the two completely independently.

Assuming we have a material balance in a position, then one of the most important features is the relative activity of the pieces. There can be an advantage for one side if he has one piece which is performing several useful functions at the same time. On the other hand, a side can be severely disadvantaged if one of his pieces is not pulling his or her weight.

We shall begin by studying the theme of outposts, as this is a subject that crops up throughout the entire book.

So what is an outpost? In fact, this isn't such an easy question because chess writers have come up with quite a few definitions over the years. The one I will use is a rather wide interpretation:

*An outpost is a square where it is possible to establish a piece which cannot easily be attacked by opposing pawns.*

To this I will add the following provisos:

1) An outpost is normally protected by one or more pawns.

2) An outpost in the centre of the board is generally more useful than one on the side.

3) An outpost in enemy territory is especially useful.

Let's try to clarify a few points by looking at an example. In this first diagram White's main outposts are at c5 and e5. The c5-square cannot easily be attacked enemy pawns (Black would first have to eliminate the a5-pawn before playing ...b7-b6).

The e5-square is the most central and

thus probably the most beneficial outpost for White, especially as there is a knight on f3 ready to hop in. This square can actually be attacked by an enemy pawn, but only after the knight on f6 moves and Black plays ...f7-f6. Black would often be reluctant to do this as it would leave extra weaknesses in his position (on e6 and g6), so in this respect the e5-square qualifies as an outpost.

Less important outposts for White are the b6 and h5-squares (obviously the placing of the pieces have some say in the matter; put Black's king on a7 and a white rook on c8 – then b6 would be White's most useful outpost, whether for queen, knight or bishop!).

Black's major outposts in this position are d5, f4 and b5. In fact, the knight on f6 is ready to hop into the d5-square. On d5 the knight is immune from attack from enemy pawns and block's white's isolated d-pawn (in our look at isolated queen's pawn positions you will see that this is a common theme). In this particular position the d5-square is an especially good outpost for the black knight; from here it can jump straight into another outpost on f4. The f4-outpost could be quite bad news for White, especially if he has castled on the kingside.

## Knights Love Outposts!

Kings, queens, rooks and bishops all like outposts, but in general the best piece for an outpost is a knight. This is due to the knight's unique jumping ability. Unlike the other pieces, a knight loses none of its power when blocking an enemy pawn, or when it's being protected by one or two of its own pawns. A knight in a secure outpost in the centre of the board and on the fifth or sixth rank can often be a decisive advantage.

Here the white knight is fantastically placed on e6, influencing events both in front and behind. Notice that the knight is particularly harmful for the black king, who cannot castle either on the kingside or queenside.

## Exploiting Outposts

An outpost is only useful if it can be occupied by a piece, otherwise it's of no real significance. However, it may not be necessary to occupy an outpost immediately. The nature of outposts is such that they are usually quite permanent, so often a player can plan many moves in advance how to exploit the square with a view to an eventually occupation. It's not an exaggeration to say that many games at grandmaster level are won and lost over one side's domination of a particular outpost. This is certainly true in the following example.

**McShane-Levitt**
Southend 2001
*French Defence*

**1 e4 e6 2 d4 d5 3 ♘d2 c5 4 ♘gf3**

cxd4 5 ♘xd4 ♘c6 6 ♗b5 ♗d7 7
♘xc6 ♗xc6 8 ♗xc6+ bxc6 9 c4

### 9...♘f6

Current theory prefers the less committal 9...♗c5, for example 10 ♕a4 ♘e7 11 cxd5 exd5 12 0-0 0-0 13 b3 ♖e8! 14 ♗b2 ♕b6 and Black has active play, Vydeslaver-Komarov, Paris 1996.

### 10 ♕a4 ♕d7 11 e5! ♘g8

11...♘g4 12 ♘f3 leaves the knight on g4 misplaced, for example 12...♗c5?! (12...h5 13 0-0 ♖b8 14 a3 ♗e7 15 b4 ♖b7 16 ♗f4 ♘h6 17 ♗xh6 ♖xh6 18 c5 was better for White in the game Ma.Tseitlin-Vaganian, USSR 1971 – the knight has a useful outpost on d4) 13 0-0 0-0 14 h3 ♘xf2 (14...♘h6 15 ♗xh6 gxh6 is also highly undesirable for Black) 15 ♖xf2 f6 16 ♗f4 ♕c7 17 ♕c2 ♕b6 18 ♖af1 ♖ac8 19 ♔h2 ♗xf2 20 ♖xf2 and predictably White's two minor pieces are worth more than Black's rook and pawn, Kengis-Votava, Prague 1993.

### 12 0-0 ♗c5?!

This runs into some trouble. 12...♘e7 13 ♘f3 ♘f5 (or 13...♘g6), and only then developing the bishop, is how Black should proceed.

### 13 ♖d1!

Threatening ♘e4. Already White has

the d6 outpost in his sights.

### 13...f5

13...♘e7 14 ♘e4! is very unpleasant for Black.

### 14 ♘b3 ♗b6 15 ♗e3!

A powerful idea. White is happy to accept doubled pawns if it means that Black's 'good bishop' is exchanged (see page 24).

### 15...♖b8

15...♗xe3 16 fxe3 ♘e7 17 ♘c5 leaves White in control of the dark squares, while the knight well posted on c5. After 17...♕c8 McShane proposes the interesting sacrifice 18 e4!? fxe4 (18...dxe4 19 ♖d6!) 19 ♖f1, which prevents Black from castling.

### 16 ♗c5!

Planning to use the d6 outpost for the bishop, while the knight will be just as happy on d4.

### 16...♘e7

16...♗xc5 17 ♘xc5 ♕c8 18 cxd5 exd5 19 ♖xd5 wins for White – McShane.

### 17 ♗d6 ♖c8 18 c5! ♗d8 19 ♕a6!

Preventing Black from playing ...a7-a5. White's eventual plan will be ♘d4, followed by b2-b4, a2-a4 and b4-b5, creating a powerful passed pawn on the queenside. It's true that Black's position is quite solid, but on the other hand he has no counterplay at all and so there is no way to fight against White's plan on the queenside.

**19...0-0 20 ♘d4 f4 21 b4 ♖f7 22 a4 ♘f5**

A minor success for Black, who at least exchanges White's powerful knight. The bishop on d6, however, remains a real thorn in the flesh.

**23 ♘xf5 ♖xf5 24 b5 ♖f7 25 b6 ♕b7 26 ♕xb7 ♖xb7 27 a5 a6**

Black is being forced to use his rook on b7 as a pawn blocker and, as McShane notes, the rook now closely resembles a big pawn! White now begins a second plan of opening the kingside, which in the long term will prove to be decisive.

One further point is that, ridiculous as it seems, strictly speaking White has the 'bad bishop' and Black possesses the 'good bishop' (see page 24). Such is the problem of using certain terms in chess!

**28 ♖a4 ♗g5 29 h4 ♗h6 30 ♖d3 ♔f7 31 g3 ♖g8 32 gxf4 g6 33 ♖g3 ♗f8 34 h5 ♖g7**

Of course capturing on d6 doesn't give Black any relief, but simply provides White with an extra protected passed pawn on the sixth rank.

**35 hxg6+ hxg6 36 ♔g2 ♖g8 37 ♖a1 ♗g7 38 ♔f3 ♖h8 39 ♖ag1 ♖h6**

Given the plight of Black's rook on b7, White is effectively playing with an extra piece on the kingside. It's no surprise that there is an immediate breakthrough.

**40 f5! exf5 41 e6+! ♔xe6 42 ♗f4 g5 43 ♖xg5 ♗f6 44 ♖e1+ ♔f7 45 ♖xf5 ♖g6 46 ♖xd5! 1-0**

An instructive finish. Following 46...cxd5 47 c6 ♖e7 48 ♖xe7+ ♗xe7 49 b7 ♖g8 50 c7, White promotes his pawns.

**The Battle over an Outpost**

Given that domination and occupation

of an outpost in enemy territory can be decisive, there are many games where the whole positional battle revolves around one specific square. In some lines of the Sicilian Defence (for example, the Najdorf), this particular battle often revolves around the d5-square. If White can secure the d5-square as an outpost, then his chances of success usually increase.

Lets look at a few typical moves in a Najdorf Sicilian.

**1 e4 c5 2 ♘f3 d6 3 d4 cxd4 4 ♘xd4 ♘f6 5 ♘c3 a6**

The move which signifies the Najdorf. This is a very common choice at grandmaster level, and is a favourite of both Bobby Fischer and Garry Kasparov.

**6 ♗c4**

This introduces the Sozin Attack, which is Fischer's own favourite weapon against his favourite defence!

**6...e6 7 0-0 ♗e7 8 ♗b3 ♕c7**

More common is 8...0-0 or 8...b5.

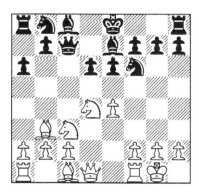

**9 f4!**

A defining moment. The advance of the f-pawn signals the beginning of a key plan for White, which is seen in many such Sicilian positions. Amongst other things, White plans the pawn lunge f4-f5, adding direct pressure to the e6-pawn, which is already attacked by both the knight on d4 and the bishop on b3. If Black is forced to play either ...e6-e5 or ...e6xf5, then the d5-square falls into White's possession. This square can be a particularly effective outpost for the knight on c3.

Note that a useful by-product of White's plan is the activation of the light-squared bishop, which current bites on the granite of the e6-pawn. If White is successful in removing this pawn, the bishop comes to life and can be used as an attacking weapon against the black king.

This type of plan was popularised by Fischer and is now seen throughout modern chess in many forms.

**9...0-0 10 f5 e5**

There is no good way to defend the pawn 10...exf5? is in no way a lesser evil because 11 ♘xf5 leaves White with another good outpost on f5, as well as the one on d5.

**11 ♘de2**

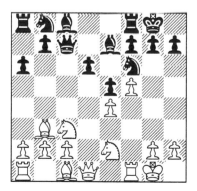

This is the correct retreat for the knight, the reasons for which will become apparent below.

From the diagram position the only thing that both White and Black are interested in is the battle for control of the d5-square, which White sees as a potentially decisive outpost. White will attempt to gain ultimate control over the square by exchanging off Black's real and potential defenders of the d5-square. Helping in the battle to control d5 will be all four of White's minor pieces. The bishop on b3 and the knight on c3 already monopolise the square; meanwhile White may attempt to exchange black knights on f6 with manoeuvres ♗g5xf6 and/or ♘g3-h5xf6 (this explains why 11 ♘de2 is stronger than say 11 ♘f3).

Similarly, Black will fight for control over the square with moves such as ...♘bd7 (supporting the knight on f6 and possibly aiming for ...♘b6), ...b7-b5-b4 (harassing the knight on c3), ...♗b7 (protecting the d5-square again) and ...♖ac8 (adding pressure down the c-file and thus forcing White to defend c2).

Let the battle commence!

**11...♘bd7**

Adding support to f6.

**12 ♗g5**

Of course this bishop cannot directly control the f6-square so it does the next best thing; eliminating a defender.

Early occupation of the outpost is not necessarily good thing – domination is the key. Nevertheless, 12 ♘d5!? is a serious option. After 12...♘xd5 13 ♗xd5 one controller from both sides have been eliminates; this is not an overall gain for the white player. Following 13...♘f6 14 ♘c3 we have:

a) 14...♗d7 (preparing ...♗c6) 15 ♔h1 (White has to be careful as the immediate 15 ♗g5?? fails to 15...♕c5+ 16 ♔h1

♘xd5 and Black wins a piece, this trick is worth remembering) 15...♗c6 16 ♗e3 (16 ♗g5!? looks like a more serious try for an advantage, for example 16...♘xd5 17 ♘xd5 ♗xd5 18 ♗xe7 ♕xe7 19 ♕xd5 with an edge to White) 16...♖ac8 17 ♕f3 ♗xd5 18 exd5

and White is left with a pawn in the d5-square. This is a good scenario for Black; d5 can no longer be occupied by a white piece and the pawn shields Black's own backward pawn on d6, which is now less vulnerable to attack.

b) 14...♖b8 (preparing ...b7-b5) 15 ♔h1 (15 ♗g5?? again loses a piece to 15...♕c5+ 16 ♔h1 ♘xd5) 15...b5 (15...h6!?, preventing ♗g5, is a possibility for Black) 16 a3 (otherwise Black plays ...b5-b4) 16...a5 17 ♗g5 b4 18 axb4 axb4 19 ♗xf6 ♗xf6 20 ♘e2 ♗b7 21 c4! and White has a slight advantage.

**12...b5**

Preparing ...♗b7 and possibly ...b5-b4.

**13 ♘g3**

This knight heads for h5 in order to exchange Black's second knight.

**13...♗b7 14 ♗xf6 ♘xf6 15 ♘h5**

*see following diagram*

**15...b4?!**

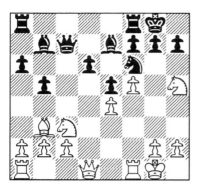

With this move Black realises he has lost the battle for control over d5 and it's just a case of damage limitation. Note that 15...♘xe4? 16 ♘xe4 ♗xe4 17 ♕g4 g6 18 ♕xe4 gxh5 19 f6 is absolutely horrible for Black

White's threat after 15 ♘h5 is 16 ♘xf6+ ♗xf6 17 ♗d5!, achieving the best case scenario – White he ends up with an unchallenged knight on the d5-square. After 17...b4 18 ♗xb7 ♕xb7 19 ♘d5 White has a huge advantage – a quick glance is sufficient to see how powerful the knight is on d5.

With this is mind, Black's best chance to confuse matters is 15...♖ac8!, which causes White some concern with the protection of his c2-pawn, for example:

a) 16 ♘xf6+ ♗xf6 17 ♖f2 (protecting the c2-pawn, but this gives White a headache on the g1-a7 diagonal; White should consider sacrificing the c-pawn with 17 ♗d5 ♗xd5 18 ♘xd5 ♕xc2 19 ♕g4 ♔h8 20 ♖f2 ♕c5 21 ♖af1) 17...♗g5 (17...♕b6 18 ♘d5 ♗xd5 19 ♗xd5 ♗g5 20 ♔f1! ♗e3 21 ♖f3 is a better version of the game for Black, but White still has an edge) 18 ♕d3 ♕c5 19 ♖e1 ♗d8! and suddenly Black obtains masses of counterplay with ...♗b6 – an

example of a 'bad bishop' becoming good!

b) 16 ♖f2!? is a worthwhile alternative – by refraining from exchanging on f6 so early, White eliminates some of Black's options: 16...♘xh5 17 ♕xh5 d5!? (preparing ...♗c5) 18 f6 (18 ♘xd5 ♗xd5 19 ♗xd5 ♗c5 20 ♖af1 ♕e7 21 g4 ♔h8 22 g5 f6 looks better for Black) 18...♗xf6 19 ♗xd5 b4 20 ♗xb7 ♕xb7 21 ♘d5 ♗e7 22 ♔h1 and I find this position difficult to evaluate. White has succeeded in posting a knight on d5, but has been forced to relinquish his spearheading pawn on f5 in exchange for Black's lowly d6-pawn. Probably 'a little better for White' is about right.

**16 ♘xf6+ ♗xf6 17 ♘d5 ♗xd5**

Or 17...♕c5+ 18 ♔h1 ♗xd5 19 ♕xd5 ♕xd5 20 ♗xd5 ♖ac8 21 ♗b3 ♖fd8 22 ♖fd1 ♖c5 23 ♔g1 a5 24 ♔f2 ♔f8 25 ♔f3 g6 26 g4 ♔e7 27 a3 bxa3 28 ♖xa3 h5 29 h3 hxg4+ 30 hxg4 gxf5 31 gxf5 ♖h8 32 ♖da1 and White went on to win in I.Almasi-Orgovan, Cansys 1991.

**18 ♕xd5**

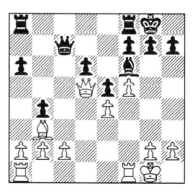

White's plan has succeeded and he holds an advantage – he dominates the d5-square, he has a stronger bishop and pressure against both d6 and f7. Black can look back at move fifteen for an improvement, while even going as far back as move eight, ...♕c7 is only semi-useful – Black may have been better advised using the tempo elsewhere.

From the diagram, the game Bhattacharyya-Suvrajit, Calcutta 1994 concluded **18...♕c5+?!** (this merely blocks the c-file and reduces Black's counterplay) **19 ♕xc5 dxc5 20 ♗d5 ♖ad8 21 a3!** (opening the a-file for the rook) **21...a5 22 axb4 axb4 23 ♖a7 ♗g5 24 ♔f2 ♖c8 25 b3 ♗d2 26 ♔e2 ♗c3 27 g4 ♗d4 28 ♖b7 ♖b8?**

**29 ♗xf7+! ♔h8 30 ♖xb8 ♖xb8 31 ♗d5 ♖d8 32 g5 ♖c8 33 h4 ♖d8 34 h5 h6 35 gxh6 ♖f8 36 ♖f3 ♔h7 37 hxg7 ♔xg7 38 ♔d3 ♔h6 39 ♖h3 ♖f6 40 ♔c4 ♔g5 41 ♗e6 ♖h6 42 ♗f7 ♔f4 1-0**

In the following game Fischer shows in quite dramatic fashion how Black can combat White's plan more successfully.

**R.Byrne-Fischer**
Sousse Interzonal 1967
*Sicilian Defence*

**1 e4 c5 2 ♘f3 d6 3 d4 cxd4 4 ♘xd4**

♘f6 5 ♘c3 a6 6 ♗c4 e6 7 ♗b3 b5

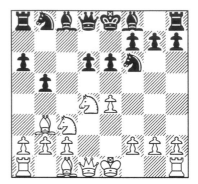

**8 f4**

Here we go again! I should point out that in this particular variation, partially as a consequence of this game, 8 0-0 ♗e7 9 ♕f3 has replaced 8 f4 as the main theoretical line these days, White generally striving for an advantage with early piece play, only aiming for f4-f5 later on (see the next game for such an example).

**8...♗b7 9 f5 e5 10 ♘de2 ♘bd7**

The pawn grab 10...♘xe4 is a bit greedy, but certainly not out of the question: 11 ♘xe4 ♗xe4 12 0-0 ♗b7 13 ♘c3 ♗e7 14 ♘d5 ♗f6 15 ♗e3 ♘d7 16 ♕h5 gave White a promising position for the pawn deficit in Dely-Bednarski, Zinnowitz 1964.

10...♗xe4? loses simply to 11 ♘xe4 ♘xe4 12 ♕d5.

**11 ♗g5 ♗e7 12 ♘g3**

Once again White prepares ♘h5.

**12...♖c8**

Adding pressure down the c-file. 12...0-0 looks natural enough, but allows White to carry out his plan: 13 ♗xf6 ♘xf6 14 ♘h5! ♕b6 15 ♘xf6+ ♗xf6 16 ♕d3 ♗g5 (White cannot castle either side, but he is still better as he will have an unopposed knight on d5) 17 ♗d5!

♖fd8 18 h4 ♗h6 19 g4 ♗f4 20 ♗xb7
♕xb7 21 g5 ♖ac8 22 ♘d5 ♖c4 23 c3
♖dc8 24 f6 ♔h8 25 fxg7+ ♔xg7 26 0-0
with a clear plus for White, Susnik-
S.Nikolic, Ljubljana 1996.

## 13 0-0?

Surprisingly enough this natural move
is a serious mistake, although this is only
shown up by the brilliance of Fischer's
next move. White has two stronger alternatives:

a) 13 ♘h5 ♘xh5 14 ♕xh5 0-0 15
♗xe7 (15 h4 b4 16 ♘d5 ♗xd5 17 exd5
♘c5 18 0-0-0 a5 19 ♕g4 a4 20 ♗c4 b3
gave Black a strong attack, R.Byrne-
Bouaziz, Sousse Interzonal 1967)
15...♕xe7 and Black has nothing to fear.
After 16 ♕e2 ♘f6 17 ♘d5 ♗xd5 18
exd5 ♖c5 a white pawn has landed onto
the crucial square – Black has won this
positional battle. Voss-Trisic, Dortmund
1992 concluded 19 c4 bxc4 20 ♗xc4
♖fc8 21 ♗b3 ♘xd5 22 ♕xa6 ♕h4+ 23
♔d1 ♕d4+ 24 ♔e2 ♕e3+ and White
resigned.

b) 13 ♗xf6 ♘xf6 14 ♘h5 is a more
direct method of trying to win the battle
for the d5-square, but Black is also well
armed against this response: 14...♖xc3! (a
typical exchange sacrifice and yet another

point of ...♖c8) 15 ♘xf6+ ♗xf6 16 bxc3
♗xe4 17 0-0 d5 18 a4 0-0 19 axb5 axb5
20 ♕e2 ♕b6+ 21 ♔h1 ♗g5 and Black
has good compensation for the exchange: a pawn, the bishop pair and
weak white pawns to aim at, Ledic-
Szabo, Vinkovci 1970.

## 13...h5!!

Characteristically it's Fischer who
finds the antidote to one of his own
plans! Black uses the very fact that he
hasn't castled to lunge forward with this
pawn, a multi-dimensional move:

1) It prevents ♘h5.

2) It prepares ...h5-h4, attacking the
knight which defends the crucial e4-
pawn.

3) It begins a surprisingly effective attack on the white kingside.

It's not too early to say that White is
already in big trouble.

## 14 h4

This move looks ugly what else is
there? 14 ♗xf6 ♘xf6 brings White no
relief after:

a) 15 ♕f3 ♖xc3! 16 ♕xc3 h4

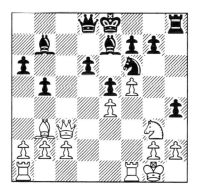

and Black has a vicious attack, for
example 17 ♘h1 ♕b6+ 18 ♘f2 ♘xe4 19
♕d3 h3! 20 g3 ♘xf2 21 ♖xf2 ♕c6 and
White is killed down the long diagonal,

or 17 ♘e2 ♛b6+ 18 ♔h1 ♘xe4 19 ♛h3
♘g5 20 ♛g4 h3 21 ♖g1 ♘e4 22 ♖af1
♘f2+ 23 ♖xf2 ♛xf2 24 ♛xg7 hxg2+ 25
♖xg2 ♛xe2 26 ♗xf7+ ♔d8 27 ♛xh8+
♔c7 and Black mates, Bednarski-
Lehmann, Palma de Mallorca 1967.

b) 15 ♘d5 h4 16 ♘xf6+ gxf6! 17 ♘h1
♗xe4 18 ♛g4 d5 and Black is already
winning. Thorsteins-Ghitescu, Reykjavik
1970 concluded 19 ♖ad1 ♗c5+ 20 ♘f2
♔e7 21 ♖fe1 ♗xf2+ 22 ♔xf2 ♛b6+ 23
♔f1 ♖hg8 24 ♛xh4 ♖xg2 and White
threw in the towel.

**14...b4**

**15 ♗xf6**

Or 15 ♘d5 ♘xd5 16 ♗xd5 ♗xg5 17
hxg5 ♗xd5 18 ♛xd5 ♛xg5 and Black is
in complete command.

**15...♗xf6**

15...♘xf6 is just as good: 16 ♘d5
♘xd5 17 ♗xd5 ♗xd5 18 ♛xd5 ♗xh4 is
horrible for White.

**16 ♘d5 ♗xh4**

And so White has control over d5, but
his kingside is fatally weakened – this is
not a good deal.

**17 ♘xh5 ♛g5**

Black now has the luxury of an open
h-file down which to attack. I guess it
could be said that White has won a battle

(of the d5-square) but has lost the war.
Byrne gamely puts up a fight but from
here on in the result is never in doubt.

**18 f6 g6 19 ♘g7+ ♔d8**

Threatening ...♗xd5, followed by
...♛e3+.

**20 ♖f3 ♗g3**

Now Black threatens ...♛h4.

**21 ♛d3 ♗h2+ 22 ♔f1 ♘c5 23 ♖h3**

23 ♛e2 ♗g3 is terminal.

**23...♖h4 24 ♛f3 ♘xb3 25 axb3
♖xh3 26 ♛xh3 ♗xd5**

White has even lost control over d5!

**27 exd5 ♛xf6+ 28 ♔e1 ♛f4 0-1**

White's pieces, especially the knight
on g7, are on silly squares. A magical
performance from Fischer.

In more recent times players have often delayed the f4-f5 advance until it can
be utilised more successfully. In the following game I decided to delay the advance; when it finally did come it was
almost instantly decisive.

**Emms-Shipov**
Hastings 1998/9
*Sicilian Defence*

**1 e4 c5 2 ♘f3 d6 3 d4 cxd4 4 ♘xd4**

♘f6 5 ♘c3 a6 6 ♗c4 e6 7 0-0 ♗e7
8 a4 ♘c6 9 ♗e3 0-0 10 ♔h1 ♗d7

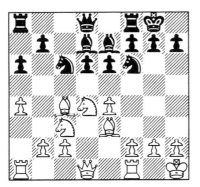

**11 f4 ♖c8**

A useful move, occupying the half-open c-file and indirectly hitting the bishop on c4.

**12 ♗a2**

Retreating the bishop to a safe haven.

**12...♕c7 13 ♕e2**

White can already consider playing the thematic 13 f5!? but I preferred to prepare by developing my queen and a1-rook.

**13...♘a5?!**

Black's idea is to occupy the c4-square with the knight, which would hit both the pawn on b2 and the bishop on e3. This is often a good plan for Black in Sicilian positions, but on this particular occasion White is well prepared – the knight on c4 actually becomes a bit of a liability. A year later, the young Russian grandmaster Alexander Grischuk came up with a solid plan for Black: 13...♘xd4 14 ♗xd4 e5! (paradoxically opening up the a2-g8 diagonal, but Black is ready to challenge immediately) 15 ♗e3 ♗e6! (neutralising White's bishop on a2) 16 a5 (or 16 f5!? ♗xa2 17 ♖xa2 ♕c4 18 ♕xc4 ♖xc4 19 ♗g5 ♖fc8 and White can dream

about exchanging on f6 and plonking a knight into d5, but with Black's pressure along the half-open c-file and e4, turning this into a reality doesn't look on the cards) 16...♗xa2 17 ♖xa2 ♕c4 18 ♕f3 (18 ♕d3? ♘xe4! wins material) 18...exf4 (18...♘xe4 19 ♖a4!) 19 ♗xf4 ♕e6 20 ♖a4 ♖c4 with an equal position, Emms-Grischuk, Esbjerg 2000 – both e4 and d6 are a little weak.

**14 ♖ad1!**

Preparing White's next move

**14...♘c4 15 ♗c1**

By moving the bishop back to its home square White solves the problem of both the bishop and the b2-pawn. Now Black's major pieces on the c-file are tied down to defending the vulnerable knight on c4, who has an uncertain future.

**15...♖fd8**

Black prepares ...♕c5. The immediate 15...♕c5 16 e5! is tactically strong for White, for example 16...dxe5 17 fxe5 ♘xe5 (17...♘e8? 18 ♘f5! is winning for White, Emms-Joachim, German Bundesliga 2000; 17...♘d5 is relatively best) 18 ♘b3 ♕c7 19 ♗f4 ♗d6 20 ♖xd6 ♕xd6 21 ♗xe5 ♕e7 22 ♗xf6 gxf6 23 ♘d5!.

**16 g4!**

Planning to evict the f6-knight from its favourite defensive square, where it protects d5. White's f4-f5 will then arrive with maximum punch. The thematic 16 f5 is not so effective yet: 16...e5 17 ♘f3 b5! and Black's counterplay arrives in time.

**16...♕c5?**

Preparing to support the knight with ...b7-b5, but Black is too late. After 16...h6 White can break through with a direct attack, for example 17 g5 hxg5 18 fxg5 ♘h7 19 ♕h5 ♘e5 20 ♖xf7!! ♘xf7 21 g6 ♘f6 22 gxf7+ ♔f8 23 ♕g6 and Black is lost – 23...♕c5 24 ♗h6! gxh6 (24...♘h5 25 ♗xe6 ♗f6 26 ♕h7) 25 ♖g1 and there is no good defence to ♕g8+.

16...e5! (Ftacnik) is Black's best chance. White keeps an edge after both 17 ♘f5 ♗xf5 18 gxf5 exf4 19 ♖xf4 and 17 fxe5 dxe5 18 ♘f5 ♗xf5 19 ♖xd8+ ♗xd8 20 ♖xf5.

**17 g5 ♘e8**

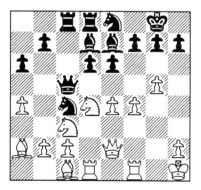

**18 f5!**

Finally the push comes and Black already has a lost position.

**18...e5**

Giving White all that he wants, but Black has no real choice, for example

18...b5 19 fxe6 fxe6 20 ♕f2 leaves White with too many attacking threats.

**19 ♘d5**

Naturally. The knight moves into the newly formed outpost with devastating effect.

**19...♗f8 20 b4 ♕a7**

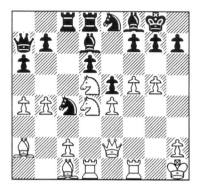

**21 ♗xc4**

And now the bishop comes back to life with a bang.

**21...exd4 22 g6**

Such was the power of f4-f5, that White can now win without having to do anything spectacular.

**22...♔h8**

Or 22...fxg6 23 ♘e7+ ♔h8 24 ♘xg6+ hxg6 25 fxg6 ♘f6 26 ♖xf6 and ♕h5+.

**23 gxf7 ♘c7 24 ♘f4 1-0**

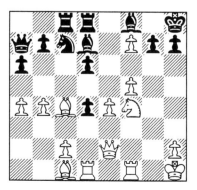

There is no good defence to the threat of 25 ♘g6+ hxg6 26 ♕g4.

### Sacrificing to Create an Outpost

Sometimes it may well be worth sacrificing material in order to secure an important outpost. Often this sacrifice comes in the form of a rook for a minor piece. Take the following example.

**Ward-Gibbs**
Caribbean Open 1999

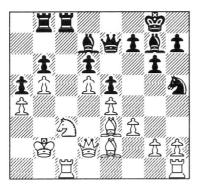

White has an advantage in this position: he has more space and can hope to utilise the open c-file. Meanwhile, the weakness of the b6-pawn is another point in White's favour.

But how can White increase the pressure? He would like to sink a piece into the juicy outpost on c6, but it seems impossible for his light-squared bishop or his knight to reach that square. Ward's method, although not entirely original, nevertheless deserves praise for its simple execution.

**21 ♘b1**

Challenging for the c-file.

**21...f5**

Predictably Black makes a typical King's Indian pawn break.

**22 ♖c6!**

This type of exchange sacrifice has been seen often, and not many Grandmasters would think too long and hard before playing such a move.

It's worth pointing out here that 22 exf5? would be a very instructive mistake, allowing Black's sleeping bishop on g7 to wake up with a timely ...e5-e4!.

**22...♗xc6**

If Black resists the offer White will simply increase the pressure on the c-file with ♖hc1.

**23 dxc6**

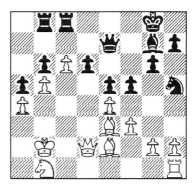

For the sacrificed material White has many advantages:

1) A powerful protected passed pawn on c6.

2) An outpost on d5.

3) Easier access to Black's backward pawn on d6.

4) The elimination of Black's best minor piece, and, as a consequence, control over the light squares.

Added up, these pluses amount to a decisive white advantage.

**23...fxe4 24 fxe4 ♘f6 25 ♘c3 ♔h8 26 ♗g5!**

By now we should be getting used to this idea. The bishop exchanges itself for

Black's final protector of f6.

**26...♕c7 27 ♗xf6 ♗xf6 28 ♗g4**

White's position is so good that he is immediately winning back material.

**28...♗g7**

28...♖f8 29 ♘d5 ♕g7 30 c7 ♖a8 31 ♖f1 is winning for White.

**29 ♘d5 ♕d8 30 ♗xc8 ♖xc8 31 ♕f2 ♕g5 32 h4 ♕h5 33 ♕f3**

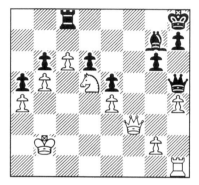

The rest of the game is very simple as far as White is concerned. He only has to exercise slight caution to prevent Black's major pieces from entering his position **33...♕h6 34 ♕e3 ♕h5 35 ♘xb6 ♖f8 36 c7 ♗h6 37 ♕f3 ♖xf3 38 gxf3 ♕xf3 39 c8♕+ ♗f8 40 ♖c1 d5 41 ♕xf8+ ♕xf8 42 ♖c8**

A powerful demonstration of the utilisation of outposts.

**The Relative Values of Outposts**

Sometimes it's the case that both sides possess and occupy outposts. When this happens the relative values of the outposts are often the most important thing. These can only be evaluated after looking at the specifics of the position, but there are some general rules. As I mentioned earlier, for example, knights tend to be the best pieces for outposts.

**Conquest-Emms**
British Championship, Eastbourne 1990

Black has the advantage in this endgame. At the moment White has to be aware of Black's attack on his front doubled c-pawn. It's true that White will be able to liquidate the pawn weakness with a timely c4-c5, but this doesn't mean the whole weakness will go away. Black will still be left in possession of the c4-square, which can prove to be a profitable outpost.

**15...♘a5 16 c5 ♗xd3+ 17 ♔xd3 bxc5 18 ♗xc5 d5!**

A very important move. Black secures the c4-square as an outpost for the knight on a5, which will be very powerfully placed. It's true that this move leaves White with a bishop well placed on another outpost on c5, but in this particular instance the knight will influence the game more than the bishop (see below).

**19 ♖ab1 ♔d7 20 e4 ♘c4**

As I said before, as a general rule, knights make better occupiers of outposts than bishops, especially when the outpost is fairly central. A reason for this is that if the bishop is supported by a pawn or two, then it has no effect on that diagonal leading backwards, whereas as the knight, being a 'jumping' piece, doesn't suffer from this problem. In this case White's bishop on c5 has no influence back on the c5-g1 diagonal. Of course this is a general rule which, depending on the specifics of a position, has many exceptions.

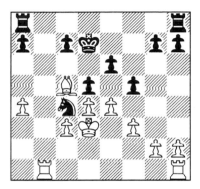

**21 ♖he1 ♖he8 22 ♖b3**

22 ♖b7 ♔c6! 23 ♖cb1? loses material to 23...♘b6!.

**22...♖ab8! 23 ♖eb1**

The plausible variation 23 ♖xb8 ♖xb8 24 ♗xa7 ♖a8 25 ♗c5 ♖xa4 26 exd5 exd5 27 ♖e7+ ♔c6 28 ♖xg7 is a graphic illustration of the power of the black knight here. Following 28...♖a2! White cannot prevent mate with ...♖d2.

**23...♖xb3 24 ♖xb3 a6 25 ♖b1**

25 ♖b7 ♔c6 26 ♖a7 a5 leaves White's rook out of play on a7. Meanwhile, Black's threat is simply ...♖b8-b2-d2!.

**25...h5 26 h3 h4**

White has the open b-file, but can do nothing with it and must wait while Black gains ground on the other wing.

**27 ♖b3**

White cannot leave the b-file: 27 ♖e1 ♖b8 28 exd5 exd5 29 ♖e7+ ♔d8 30 ♖xg7 ♖b2 31 ♗e7+ ♔e8 32 ♗g5 ♖xg2

is good for Black – the threat is ...f5-f4!.

**27...g5 28 ♖b1 ♖g8**

Planning to break through with ...g5-g4. Black's position is very easy to play.

**29 ♖e1 fxe4+ 30 fxe4 g4! 31 exd5 exd5 32 ♖e7+ ♔c6 33 ♖e6+ ♔b7 34 hxg4 ♖xg4 35 ♖e2**

**35...♖g3+ 36 ♔c2 ♖xg2!**

Winning the game with a simple tactic. It's noticeable that the influence of the black knight stretches to g2, whereas White's bishop now looks distinctly out of the game.

**37 ♖xg2 ♘e3+ 38 ♔d2 ♘xg2 39 ♔e2 h3 40 ♔f3 ♘f4 41 ♔g3 ♘e2+ 42 ♔xh3 ♘xc3 43 a5 ♔c6 44 ♔g4 ♔b5 0-1**

Of course, after all that I have said, it may be a little easy to get carried away with outposts. Sometimes, despite a powerful appearance, a piece may be stuck in an outpost with little relevance to where the main action is. Take the following example.

**Korchnoi-Kasparov**
Amsterdam 1991

Here Korchnoi is ready jump his

knight into the impressive looking c6-outpost. However, the real action is taking place on the kingside and the sad fact is that the knight on c6, pretty though it looks, actually takes no part in the game.

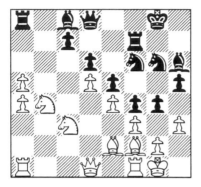

**22 ♘c6?! ♛f8 23 fxg4 hxg4 24 hxg4**

24 ♗xg4 ♘xg4 25 hxg4 f3! (Kasparov) also gives Black a strong attack.
**24...♗g5 25 ♗f3 ♛h6 26 ♖e1 ♘h4! 27 ♗xh4**

Or 27 ♔f1 ♘xf3 28 gxf3 ♘xg4! 29 fxg4 f3 and Black has a winning attack.
**27...♗xh4 28 g5?!**

White's last chance is to give up the exchange with 28 ♔f1.
**28...♛xg5 29 ♖e2 ♘g4 30 ♖b1 ♗g3 31 ♛d3 ♛h4 0-1**

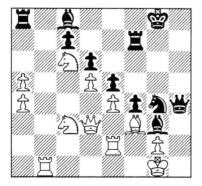

And all the time the knight on c6 looks on from its perch as an impressed spectator.

### Outposts: A Modern View

As a final thought on this subject, let's take a look at the opening moves of the main line Sveshnikov Sicilian, one of the most popular openings in modern times and a favourite of Brain Games World Champion Vladimir Kramnik (when he's taking a well-deserved break from the super-solid Berlin Defence).

**1 e4 c5 2 ♘f3 ♘c6 3 d4 cxd4 4 ♘xd4 ♘f6 5 ♘c3 e5 6 ♘db5 d6 7 ♗g5 a6 8 ♘a3 b5 9 ♗xf6 gxf6 10 ♘d5**

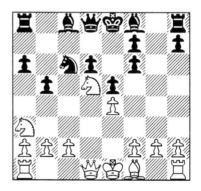

Up until the 1970s only a handful of master games had ever reached this position, with results overwhelmingly in White's favour. It looks like Black has committed positional suicide. He has gifted White an outpost on d5, where the knight is beautifully posted and unchallenged. Furthermore, Black's f-pawns are doubled and the f5-square is another potential outpost for White.

This is not the whole story, however. In the 1970s players such as Russia's

Evgeny Sveshnikov began to realise the dynamic possibilities for Black (hence the name of the opening). Black can still fight for the control of d5 with moves such as ...♗e6 and, after a preparatory ...♗g7, ...♘e7. Furthermore, Black possesses the bishop pair, which may prove to be an advantage if the position opens up. Another positive factor for Black is his mass of central pawns and his chances to undermine White's centre with ...f6-f5. Last, but certainly not least, White has had to pay some price for inducing the weakness on d5: White's knight on a3 is by far the worst piece on the board and it will take White some time to relocate back to a useful square.

Black, of course, can utilise this time by getting his own counterplay up and running.

So, in conclusion, outposts are an important aspect of positional play and you should always be careful about loose pawn moves which can create outposts for your opponent (remember pawns can never move backwards!). On the other hand, outposts are still only one aspect of the game and thus can only be judged along with the specifics of a certain position. After all, it's no use having a juicy outpost for your knight on the queenside, when the horse would be better off trying to stave off a mating attack on the other wing!

# CHAPTER TWO

## Pieces:
## The Good, the Bad and the Ugly

Now we have dealt with subject of outposts we are in a much better position to appreciate the relative value of certain pieces. Of particular importance in the middlegame is the value of the minor pieces (bishops and knights) and we shall begin by taking a look at some examples of these.

### 'Good Bishops' and 'Bad Bishops'

The terms 'good bishop' and 'bad bishop' are etched in stone in the history of chess literature. Unfortunately, as we shall see, the terms are a little misleading. A 'good bishop' is often very effective, but can on occasions be very ineffective. At the same time, a 'bad bishop' is often just plain bad, but it *can* be very effective too, both in attack and for defensive purposes ('bad bishops protect good pawns' is one of grandmaster Mihai Suba's more cryptic remarks).

Confused? Then perhaps we should try to clarify a few things by looking at a few basic examples.

Here is a typical pawn structure arising from the French Defence (1 e4 e6 2 d4

d5 3 e5 say). Also on the board we can see all four bishops.

Starting with White's light-squared bishop on d3. This is a classical example of a 'good bishop' and it's very effectively placed, attacking down the long b1-h7 diagonal. The bishop is termed as 'good' because White's pawns, especially the ones on the central files, do not obstruct the path of the bishop, as they are on different coloured squares. Similarly, Black's bishop on e7 is also an example of an effective 'good bishop' – Black's bishop moves on dark squares while the e6- and d5-pawns are on light squares.

Now we move to the 'bad bishops'. Black's light-squared bishop is 'bad' because the pawns in the centre obstruct its path. In fact, the light-squared bishop is one of Black major problems in many lines of the French. In this position the bishop on d7 is the worst placed bishop on the board. It does provide some defensive duties, but it's hampered by lack of the e6- and d5-pawns, plus a lack of space.

White's bishop on c1 is also termed as a 'bad bishop'. However, owing to White's greater space advantage, this bishop is quite not as badly placed as the one on d7. It does, after all, control some important squares on the kingside.

If we were now to move White's f-pawn to f4 and Black's f-pawn to f5, then there would be a slight change in values. White's bishop on c1 would be further hampered by the f4-pawn, while the prospects of the d7-bishop are improved on account of the possible manoeuvre ...♗d7-e8-h5.

how effective it is on d5. The point is that a 'bad' bishop can become extremely powerful if it can locate itself on the outside of the pawn chain, as on this occasion. Then the fact that it has pawns on the same colour can be a help, as the bishop is more likely to find a desirable outpost. Of course, the bishop's future would be somewhat bleaker if it were locked away, for example, on e2.

Now we come to White's 'good bishop' on b2. Except that we can clearly see its lack of effectiveness! I would call this bishop 'ugly'. On this occasion it's the black pawn structure that has smothered the bishop's range. By gaining space and putting his pawns on dark squares, Black has managed to minimise the power of White's 'good bishop' (at a cost of some light square control, it should be said).

### 'Good' and 'Bad' Bishops in Action
We begin by studying a classic case of an effective 'good bishop' against an ineffective 'bad bishop'.

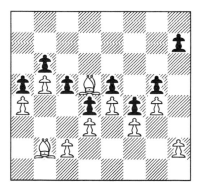

In this second example we see the problem with the usage of the terms 'good' and 'bad'. Technically speaking, the light-squared bishop on d5 is 'bad', but only a fool would fail to appreciate

### Shirov-Short
Sarajevo 2000

This position arose from a typical

French Defence that has gone wrong for Black. The two most distinctive features are the superiority of White's 'good bishop' over Black's 'bad bishop' and Black's vulnerable backward e6-pawn on the half-open e-file. Add these two together and there's no doubt that White has a clear advantage.

But how does White to make progress? It's quite instructive how Shirov goes about exploiting these pluses.

**20 ♘e5!**

By exchanging knights White rids the position of some 'impurities', which highlights even more Black's main two problems. And I haven't mentioned yet the outpost on e5.

**20...♘xe5 21 ♖xe5 ♖ef7**

Black would love to swing his bishop around via e8 to the kingside, where it could begin to work effectively outside the pawn chain. However, the weakness on e6 makes this manoeuvre impossible, for example 21...♗e8 22 ♖fe1 ♗g6? 23 ♗xd5! wins material.

**22 f4**

Cementing down the e5-outpost.

**22...♕h6 23 h4**

A useful move as White may wish to increase the pressure on the e6-pawn with ♗h3.

**23...♖f5 24 ♖e3 ♕g6 25 ♔h2 ♖5f6 26 ♖fe1 ♖e8 27 ♖1e2 ♕f7 28 ♕e1**

White trebles on the e-file and increases the pressure on e6. The position looks grim for Black, but grandmasters often talk about the fact that one weakness on its own is not normally enough to win or lose a game. Unless Black does something silly, White will have to create another point of attack in order to be successful.

**28...♔f8 29 ♗h3 h5 30 ♖e5 g6**

Gaining some much needed space on the kingside but, on the other hand, fixing yet another two pawns on light squares. This doesn't help Black's poor bishop in the long term.

**31 ♕b1 ♔g7 32 ♕b4**

Black is just about holding on the kingside, so Shirov tries something on the other wing. The idea is to open the position up with a3-a4-a5.

**32...♕f8 33 a4**

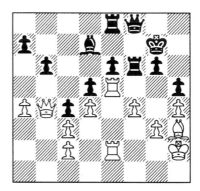

**33...♕xb4?**

It's understandable that Black wanted to relieve some of the pressure by exchanging queens, but this comes at a price of straightening out White's only weakness – the doubled c-pawns. Black should have probably tried waiting, even if this allows White to arrange a4-a5.

**34 cxb4 a6**

34...≜xa4 allows 35 ≜xe6, after which the d5-pawn also drops.

**35 c3 ≜f7 36 ≖a2 ≜e7**

It might be worth Black considering 36...a5 here. If White blocks with b4-b5 then Black does not have the worries of the weak a6/b5 pawns as in the game. Also, the line 37 bxa5 bxa5 38 ≖b2 ≜xa4 39 ≖a2 ≜c6 40 ≖xa5 ≖a8 doesn't seem to increase White's advantage.

**37 ≜g2 ≜d6 38 ≜f3 ≖ef8 39 ≜d1 ≜e8 40 ≖f2 ≖h8 41 a5 b5**

Black has successfully blocked everything up on the queenside and now hopes that the one weakness on e6 will not be enough for White to win. However, there is now a new weakness – the pawn on a6!

**42 g4**

Finally Shirov makes a break on the kingside.

**42...hxg4 43 ≜g3 ≖ff8 44 ≜xg4 ≜f7 45 ≜g5 ≜e7 46 ≜f3 ≖fg8 47 ≖fe2 ≖h5+**

A nice trick, but of course White doesn't have to take the rook.

**48 ≜g4**

48 ≜xh5? gxh5+ 49 ≜h6 ≜f6 is certainly not what White has spent all his time preparing for. Black has a draw by perpetual with 50 ≜h7 ≖g7+ 51 ≜h6 ≖g8.

**48...≜f6 49 ≜g3 ≖hh8 50 ≜g4 ≖e8**

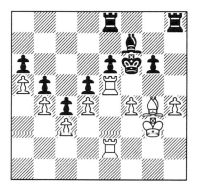

A crucial moment. Black seems to be holding on, but some imaginative play by Shirov is enough to emphasise the difference between the two bishops.

**51 h5!**

An excellent move. White sacrifices a pawn in order to make a breakthrough with f4-f5.

**51...gxh5 52 ≜h3 h4+ 53 ≜h2 ≖e7**

Or 53...≖hg8 54 f5 exf5 55 ≖xf5+ ≜g7 56 ≖g2+ ≜f8 57 ≖gf2 ≖e7 58 ≖f6 (Psakhis) and either the d5- or the a6-pawn is doomed. One possible continuation is 58...≖a7 59 ≜e6 ≖g7 60 ≜xd5 ≜e8 61 ≜xf7+ ≖gxf7 62 ≖xf7 ≖xf7 63 ≖xf7 ≜xf7 64 ≜h3 and White wins the ending.

**54 f5!**

The final breakthrough

**54...≖he8 55 ≖g2 ≜g8**

Or 55...exf5 56 ≖xf5+ ≜e6 57 ≖g7 (Psakhis) and White wins a piece, for example 57...≜g8 58 ≖ff7+ ≜d6 59 ≖xe7 ≖xe7 60 ≖xg8.

**56 ♖g6+ ♔f7 57 ♖gxe6 ♔f8**

57...♖xe6 58 fxe6+ ♔e7 59 ♖xd5 ♗xe6 60 ♖e5 ♔f7 61 ♗xe6+ ♖xe6 62 ♖xe6 ♔xe6 63 ♔h3 again leads to a winning pawn ending for White.

**58 ♖xe7 ♖xe7 59 ♖xe7 ♔xe7**

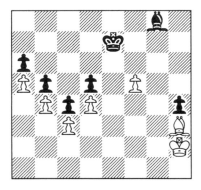

**60 f6+! 1-0**

So it's the weak a6-pawn which finally settles the game. Black is lost after 60 f6+ ♔xf6 61 ♗c8 ♗e6 62 ♗xa6 ♔e7 (or 62...♗d7 63 ♗b7) 63 ♗xb5, for example 63...♔d6 64 ♗e8 ♔c7 65 b5 ♔b7 66 ♗c6+ ♔a7 67 ♔g2 h3+ 68 ♔h2 and Black is in zugzwang.

In the next example once again it is the relative value of the minor pieces which is of utmost importance.

**Emms-Degraeve**
Gent 2001

My position play leading up to the diagram was certainly poor enough to be unpublishable and now I was about to suffer horribly for my sins. Black's main two advantages in this position are his dominant control of the dark squares and the possession of two good minor pieces to one. The odd minor piece out

is my excuse for a bishop on g4. My pawns, all on light squares, have been particularly unkind to the bishop, which now resembles nothing more than a big pawn.

**35...♕f6**

A good, logical move, which prepares to exchange bishops with ...♗d4.

**36 ♖f3 ♖a8**

Black is coming 'round the back'.

**37 ♖h3 ♖a1+ 38 ♔f2**

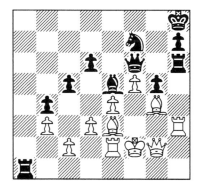

**38...♗d4!**

You might ask why Black would want to exchange his bishop which, although traditionally 'bad', is performing just as good a role as its opponent on e3. By trading bishops, however, Black 'purifies' the position, leaving the good minority piece count as 1-0 to Black, which percentage-wise, is far better than 2-1. In plain terms, Black will be left with a monstrous knight against a miserable bishop.

One final point is that the e5-square is a very nice outpost for Black, but only one piece can occupy it at a time. By exchanging the bishop Black can now occupy e5 with the knight. Legendary Russian trainer and writer Mark Dvoretsky referred to this problem as having a superfluous piece.

**39 ≜xh6 ♕xh6 40 ♕h3 ♘e5!**

In time trouble, I missed this tactic. Now White's only chance to stay in the game is with 41 ♔g3.

**41 ♕h5? ♘xg4+**

It almost seems criminal to give up the knight for the sad bishop, but on this occasion it's the quickest way to win.

**42 ♕xg4 ♕h2+ 43 ♕g2 ♕f4+! 44 ♕f3**

**44...≜f1+! 0-1**

### The Weakest Link

So far we've mainly seen the good side of knights, enjoying both having outposts and being in the centre of the board. The fact that a knight enjoys be-

ing in the centre is no secret. It's just a question of mathematics – in the centre the knight controls eight squares while on the edge the knight controls only four.

I wouldn't go quite as far as constantly repeating the old adage, 'knights on the rim are grim', but as an example I will refer you back to White's miserable beast on a3 in the Sveshnikov Sicilian (see page 22). As well as this, however, I should point out that there are many examples of a knight performing useful functions on the edge, just as it can in the centre.

Going back to the importance of minor pieces in the middlegame, the following game is a another example of 'just one bad piece spoiling it for the rest'.

**Emms-Miralles**
Andorra 1998

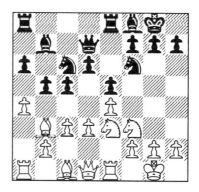

A typical position reached from the Ruy Lopez, in which I have played the restrained d2-d3, rather than aiming for d2-d4 as in the main lines. White probably has a small edge, as he has good control over d5, the only real outpost in the entire position. There is, however, nothing wrong with Black's position. He certainly has enough space, while he is ready to contest control of the d5-square with ideas such as ...♘e7, ...♘a5 or ...♘d8-e6.

**16 ♘d5**

Forcing Black to act immediately due to the twin threat of ♘b6 and ♘xf6+, weakening black's kingside pawns.

Waiting with something like 16 h3?! allows 16...♘e7! and Black is fine. The knight can go to g6 and Black can aim for the space gaining ...d6-d5.

**16...♘xd5 17 ♗xd5 ♘a5?!**

It's very natural that Black should both try to exchange the bishop on d5 and contest the d5-square, but this move is the cause of Black's problems for the rest of the game. 17...♘e7! is correct.

**18 axb5 axb5 19 b4! ♗xd5**

Black has no real choice, as after the illogical looking 19...♘c6 (what was the point of ...♘a5?) White can use the powerfully placed bishop to start a devastating attack with 20 ♘g5! ♖xa1 (the Swedish grandmaster Tom Wedberg gives 20...♖e7 21 ♖xa8 ♗xa8 22 ♕h5 h6 23 ♖e3! cxb4 24 ♖h3 – threatening ♕g6 – 24...♔h8 25 ♗xf7 and White wins) 21 ♕h5 h6 22 ♗xf7+ ♔h8 23 ♕g6! hxg5 24 ♕h5 mate.

**20 exd5 ♘b7 21 ♗e3**

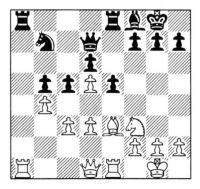

From what we have already seen regarding outposts it might, at first sight, seem that Black has done well out of the recent skirmish. After all, the d5-square is now occupied by a white pawn, which is no substitute for a piece. On this occasion, however, there is one overriding feature of the position – the awful placing of Black's knight on b7. In this respect the white pawns on b4 and d5 are doing a grand job, not allowing the knight to re-enter the game. The only square the knight currently has available is d8, but where is it going from there?

Put the knight on any sensible square and Black would be doing absolutely fine. With the knight on b7, Black has a long-term positional disadvantage. Such small positional details can be vitally important when assessing positions.

I should add that this idea of exploiting a bad knight in the Lopez was nothing original – I had already learned from both classic examples and personal experience.

**21...♕f5 22 ♕d2?!**

It would have been very nice if I had followed up my earlier good work correctly, but in fact I start to drift a little around here, perhaps content that the non-player on b7 had given me an 'extra piece', or at least a long term 'power play'. On the other hand, the very fact that White can play inaccurately and still keep a plus says something about the position.

22 ♕e2! is more logical, reserving the d2-square for the knight. Black is under no immediate pressure, but let's just play a few natural-looking moves: 22...♖ec8 23 h3 ♖xa1 24 ♖xa1 cxb4 25 cxb4 ♖c3 (why not?) 26 ♖a7! ♘d8 27 g4! and if

now 27...♕xd3 28 ♕xd3 ♖xd3 White plays 29 ♖d7 and the knight is a goner. It's not quite the end of the story, but after 29...f5 30 ♖xd8 f4 31 ♘g5! fxe3 32 ♘e6 White comes out a piece up.

**22...h6**

The immediate 22...g6!?, preparing ...♗g7, is another option but I can understand why my opponent wanted to eliminate ideas of ♘g5. After 23 ♘g5! ♗g7 24 ♘e4 (pressurising c5) 24...cxb4 25 cxb4 ♕d7 26 ♗h6 ♗h8 27 ♕g5 f5 28 ♘f6+ ♗xf6 29 ♕xf6 ♕f7 30 ♕xf7+ ♔xf7 31 ♖ec1 ♖a4 32 h4 ♔g8 33 ♖ab1 the simplification has not helped Black. If anything, the weak link on b7 is even more apparent.

**23 ♕e2**

Admitting that my previous move was a bit thoughtless!

**23...♗e7 24 h3 ♗f6 25 ♘d2 ♕g6**

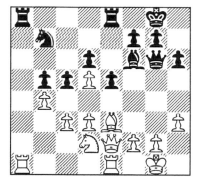

**26 ♖ab1?**

A silly move. By introducing indirect pressure on the b5-pawn, I was trying to induce my opponent into exchanging on b4, with the result being an open c-file on which White could operate, but this was no justification for giving up the open a-file.

26 ♘e4! ♗e7 27 ♕g4! ♕xg4 28 hxg4

gives White a very pleasant ending. Note how the g4-pawn prevents Black from chasing the knight with ...f7-f5. After 28...cxb4 29 cxb4 ♖a4 30 ♖xa4 bxa4 31 ♖a1 ♖a8 32 ♘c3 a3 33 ♗c1 the a-pawn is a lost, while all the time the b7-knight is a spectator.

**26...♖a2!**

Of course!

**27 ♖ed1**

27 bxc5?! tries to trade in one advantage for another. The knight is released from its hell for the price of the pawn. On this occasion, though, White is cashing in too early: 27...♘xc5 28 ♗xc5 dxc5 29 ♖xb5 c4! 30 dxc4? ♗g5 31 ♖d1 ♕c2! and Black wins a piece.

**27...e4**

Suddenly Black has real counterplay.

**28 d4**

Correctly blocking things up. After 28 dxe4 c4! Black has threats of both ...♗xc3 and ...♖xe4.

**28...c4 29 ♕g4! ♗g5!?**

My opponent does his best to keep the position complicated, aware that simplification with 29...♕xg4!? 30 hxg4 highlights the weakness of Black's knight again. White will follow up by challenging for the a-file with ♖a1, when the weakness on e4 also gives Black problems However, with active play Black can keep in the game: 30...♗g5! 31 ♗xg5 hxg5 32 ♘f1! (32 ♖a1 ♖c2! 33 ♖a7 ♖e7 is unclear) 32...♖ea8 33 ♖e1 ♖c2 34 ♖a1! ♖a4 35 ♖xa4 bxa4 36 ♖a1 ♖xc3 37 ♖xa4 ♖b3 38 ♘d2 ♖d3 39 ♘xc4 ♖xd4 40 ♘b6 and still Black has problems with his knight.

**30 ♕d7**

30 ♗xg5 hxg5? 31 ♕d7 is very good for White, as Black is forced into playing

the ugly 31...♖b8. However, Black has the very useful zwischenzug 30...f5!.

**30...♖e7 31 ♕c8+ ♔h7**

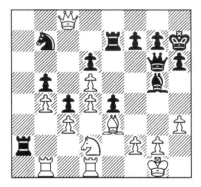

An important moment in the game. Black's knight on b7 is still by far the worst piece on the board, but as a consequence of my 26th move Black has quite a lot of action elsewhere. In particular, he threatens to go onto the offensive on the kingside with a quick ...f7-f5-f4, which looks very dangerous for White. Here I decided to offer a pawn sacrifice in order to solve the problem on the kingside.

**32 ♖a1! ♖xa1 33 ♖xa1 f5?**

Going for broke on the kingside but White gets in first 'round the back'. Black should take the pawn on offer with 33...♗xe3 34 fxe3 ♕g5 35 ♘f1 ♕xd5 but I was quite happy to play this position – it's now White who has the initiative and Black has still to solve the problem of the b7-knight (move the queen, play ...d6-d5 and finally the knight has a square on d6!): 36 ♘g3! ♕g5 (36...♕e6 37 ♕xe6 ♖xe6 38 ♖a7) 37 ♕f5+ ♕xf5 38 ♘xf5 ♖d7 39 d5! and White is still better, despite the minus pawn.

**34 ♖a8**

With an immediate threat of mate.

**34...♕f7**

34...♕f6 35 ♗xg5 ♕xg5 36 h4! ♕h5 37 ♘f1! f4 38 g4! wins for White, for example 38...♕xh4 39 ♕f5+ g6 40 ♕f8 ♕xg4+ 41 ♘g3 ♕d1+ 42 ♔g2 ♕f3+ 43 ♔h3 and Black cannot avoid mate.

**35 ♗xg5 hxg5 36 g4!**

Giving the white queen use of the h5-square and simply threatening gxf5 followed by mate on h8.

**36...fxg4 37 hxg4?**

In a perfect world and perhaps with more time I would have seen 37 ♕h8+ ♔g6 38 ♖f8 ♕xd5 39 hxg4 and Black has no escape, for example 39...♖f7 40 ♘xe4! ♖xf8 41 ♕h5 mate. However, that would have robbed me of an instructive finish!

**37...e3 38 fxe3 ♖xe3 39 ♕h8+ ♔g6 40 ♕h5+ ♔f6 41 ♕xf7+ ♔xf7 42 ♖b8**

We've simplified into an ending and Black's weak knight on b7 has finally come back to haunt him. Black's next move is forced.

**42...♖e7 43 ♔f2 ♔g6 44 ♘b1 1-0**

A nice finish. Black is virtually paralysed, his knight still cannot move and White can simply continue with ♘a3xb5.

Indeed, my opponent saw no reason to continue.

Okay, this was by no means a perfect performance, but it's interesting that once Black's knight was consigned to b7, I could even afford a couple of lapses and still keep control. I always had the comforting thought that I was playing with an extra piece.

### Don't Open the Cage Door!

In the previous example I bent over backwards to make sure that Black's poor knight could not re-enter the action. Perhaps I had learnt from previous experience, when after having done all the hard work, I would spoil it all with just one thoughtless move.

**Baker-Emms**
British League 1996

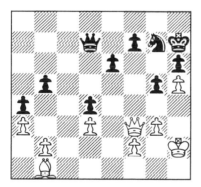

One glance at the diagram position should be enough to spot the overwhelming problem with White's position (apart from the minus pawn). That's right! The miserable looking bishop on b1. It's blocked by the d3-pawn on the b1-h7 diagonal, Black's pawns are doing a great job of restricting life on the a2-g8 diagonal and it will take a while for it to

reach the long h1-a8 diagonal; even then, it's only hitting thin air. All this makes my next move all the more incomprehensible.

**40...f5??**

Looking back at the game now, I can't believe I actually played this positional blunder. I think I was in mild time trouble, but this is really no excuse. I would certainly like to think that I wouldn't repeat this kind of mistake. The crucial point is that Black should be looking to convert his advantage without significantly changing the pawn structure, thus giving White no chance of counterplay. Objectively speaking ...f7-f5 probably doesn't quite deserve a double question mark, as Black is now clearly better as opposed to winning, but then again, there are many easier ways for Black to win and now he has to think hard again.

A rearrangement with 40...♘e8 41 ♗c2 ♔g7 42 ♗d1 ♘f6 looks like a good start for Black, for example 43 ♕e2 (43 ♕a8 ♕c7 and now there's already a threat of ...♕c1) 43...♕d5, intending ...g5-g4 and ...♕xh5.

**41 ♗a2!**

Suddenly the bishop is right back into the game. The pawn on f7 was a crucial part of locking the white bishop out, but now all the previous good work has been lost. It's true that Black can round up the h5-pawn, but in return the e6-pawn is a weakness. Moving it with ...e6-e5 will only give White all sorts of undeserved counterplay along the now vulnerable a2-g8 diagonal.

**41...♕e8 42 ♔g1 ♘xh5 43 ♗xe6 ♕xe6 44 ♕xh5**

and I failed to convert this, by now, difficult endgame.

ture – the open d-file.

## Rank and File

So far we haven't paid too much close attention to rooks, so it's about time that the balance was readdressed.

Rooks, of course, like open files; their influence in the game is dictated by this. Rooks are usually slow out of the blocks and are not often seen in the thick of the action in the opening and the early middlegame. Normally rooks come into their own once a few pieces have been exchanged and the position opens – they are especially effective in the endgame.

## Controlling an Open File

Often there is one completely open file on the board and this becomes the focus of attention for both sides. This is particularly the case if either side has a potential infiltration point into the enemy camp along the open file. In this case the battle for the control of the file becomes very significant. Take the following example.

### Ernst-Nordstrom
Avesta 1995

In a typically quiet-looking position, White attempts to control the main fea-

**18 ♖d4!**

A good start. White gains a tempo on the black knight and prepares to double rooks on the open d-file.

**18...♘f6 19 ♖fd1 ♖ac8?**

Black has to contest the open file. In his notes to the game, Ernst gives 19...♖fd8 and assesses the position as slightly better for White. White can continue with 20 ♘e5, when 20...♖xd4?! 21 ♖xd4 ♖d8?? fails to the trick 22 ♘c6!. Instead Black should cover the c6-square with 20...♕c7!.

**20 ♘e5 ♖c7**

Black already has to watch out for infiltration ideas involving the d7-square, hence his last move. 20...♖fd8? allows 21 ♘c6!, while after 20...♕c7 21 ♘d7! ♘xd7 22 ♖xd7 ♕b8 23 ♕d3 White has complete domination of the d-file.

**21 c4**

An excellent move, galvanising the queenside pawn majority (see page 111) and preventing Black from blocking the d-file with ...♘d5. White now holds a clear advantage.

**21...♖fc8 22 ♕d3 g6 23 a3 ♕c5 24 ♕e3 ♔g7 25 b4 ♕e7 26 h3 ♕e8 27 ♖d6 ♕e7 28 ♕d4**

Black is being reduced to total passivity.

**28...♔g8**

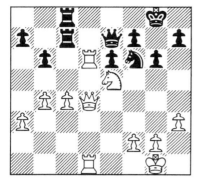

**29 b5!**

Securing the c6-square as an excellent outpost for both rook and knight.

**29...♕f8 30 ♖d3**

Slowly the net is closing in on the black position. White now has options of swinging the rook along the third rank to the f3-square.

**30...♘d5 31 ♖c6 ♘e7**

Or 31...♘f6 32 ♖f3 and Black has no good defence against the threats, for example:

a) 32...♔g7 33 ♖xf6 ♔xf6 34 ♘d7+.

b) 32...♕g7 33 ♖xc7 ♖xc7 34 ♕d8+.

c) 32...♖xc6 33 ♘xc6 ♘e8 34 ♘xa7.

**32 ♖xc7 ♖xc7 33 ♘d7**

Now the check ♘f6+ will be devastating.

**33...♕c8 34 ♘f6+ ♔f8 35 ♘xh7+ ♔g8 36 ♘f6+ ♔f8 37 ♕d8+ 1-0**

37...♕xd8 38 ♖xd8+ ♔g7 39 ♘e8+ wins the rook.

**Lobron-Makarichev**
Solingen 1991

This example is similar to the last in that White dominates the only open file. But how does White make progress? How can he infiltrate Black's position before Black has time to negate White's pressure with ...♔f8-e7 and ...♖d8? The d6-square is available to White, but it's not clear what White achieves with a rook on d6. He could try the manoeuvre ♖d6-c6-c7, but Black can easily prevent such an idea with ...♖c8.

Ideally, White would like to penetrate via the d7-square, but this is currently covered by Black's useful defensive knight on f6. The answer? Simply trade knights!

**27 ♘e4!**

Now Black has no useful way to stop the rooks from infiltrating.

**27...e5!**

Black correctly aims for some counterplay by opening the e-file. After 27...♘xe4 28 ♔xe4 White will continue with ♖d7.

**28 ♘xf6 ♔xf6 29 ♖e4!**

Threatening ♖d6+, so Black's next move is forced. 29 ♖d7 exf4 30 ♔xf4 g5+ 31 ♔f3 ♖e6 isn't so clear as Black has counterplay when he doubles rooks on the e-file.

**29...exf4 30 ♖xf4+**

**30...♔g7**

30...♔e7!? prevents an immediate occupation of d7 but after 31 ♖fd4! ♖ad8 (what else?) 32 ♖xd8 ♖xd8 33 ♖xd8 ♔xd8 34 ♔e4 it looks like a winning king and pawn ending as White's king is so dominant, for example 34...♔e7 35 ♔e5 a5 36 a3 g5 37 g4 hxg4 38 hxg4 f6+ 39 ♔f5 ♔f7 40 b4 and White wins.

**31 ♖d7 ♖f8**

Now Black is completely tied up.

**32 h4! a6**

This imperceptible weakness left on the queenside is decisive. However, even with a waiting move such as 32...♔g8, White still comes up with his king: 33 ♔e4 ♖ae8+ 34 ♔d4 and now 34...♖d8 fails to the trick 35 ♖fxf7!.

**33 ♔e4!**

White heads for the vulnerable queenside pawns.

**33...♖ae8+ 34 ♔d5 ♖e3 35 ♔c6 ♖xg3**

Or 35...♖e6+ 36 ♔b7 (Stohl), intending b3-b4 and c4-c5.

**36 ♔xb6**

At first sight it seems as if Black has undeserved counterplay but in the race for promotion White's c-pawn is far ahead of anything Black has.

**36...♖g4 37 ♖xg4 hxg4 38 c5 g5**

38...g3 simply loses the advanced pawn to 39 ♖d3.

**39 hxg5 ♔g6**

**40 c6 1-0**

40...♔xg5 41 c7 ♖c8 42 ♖xf7 is easily winning.

**When to Open a File**

Sometimes the structure of the pawns dictate that one side can open a file at any moment. The timing of such an opening, however, can be very crucial. On occasions it's better for the player in control to keep the tension as long as possibly, only opening the file when it suits him the most. The next example is a case in point.

**Fischer-Spassky**
Sveti Stefan (1st matchgame) 1992

There is a state of tension on the queenside that favours White in this position. Naturally Black does not want to capture on a4, as this would leave him with two isolated pawns on c4 and a6 (the one on c4 would be particularly difficult to defend). White can open the a-file any time he wishes with axb5, but this would then allow Black to contest the file with his own major pieces. Instead Fischer correctly uses the tension to his advantage.

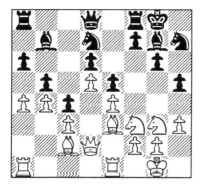

**22 ♖a3!**

A simple, but very effective move. White prepares to double rooks on the a-file although, as you will see later, this isn't the end of his ambitions. I would have said that this is exactly the sort of move that a computer would fail to appreciate, except that Deep Blue astounded everyone by playing in exactly the same manner in its famous match against Kasparov.

**22...♘df6 23 ♖ea1 ♕d7 24 ♖1a2 ♖fc8 25 ♕c1 ♗f8 26 ♕a1!**

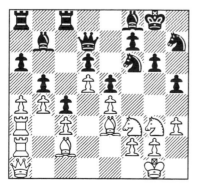

The tripling procedure is complete.

This idea was first introduced at the highest level by Alexander Alekhine, who performed a very similar procedure in a game against Aron Nimzowitsch.

White now threatens to capture on b5, so Black has to reinforce his rook on a8. **26...♕e8 27 ♘f1 ♗e7 28 ♘1d2 ♔g7 29 ♘b1!**

Brilliant play. By manoeuvring the knight to b1, Fischer is trying to exploit the weakness on b5. White's threat is simply to exchange with 30 axb5 axb5 31 ♖xa8 ♖xa8 32 ♖xa8 ♕xa8 33 ♕xa8+ ♗xa8 34 ♘a3 and the b-pawn is lost. In fact Black has no good defence against this idea, so Spassky decided to lash in the centre with a desperate sacrifice. **29...♘xe4!? 30 ♗xe4 f5 31 ♗c2 ♗xd5**

Black now has some counterplay, but objectively he must be lost. Fischer, playing his first serious game for twenty years, doesn't disappoint his fans. **32 axb5 axb5 33 ♖a7 ♔f6 34 ♘bd2 ♖xa7 35 ♖xa7 ♖a8**

**36 g4!**

Breaking up the black pawn structure and exposing the black king. It looks risky to open up the kingside, but Fischer shows that it's completely justified.

**36...hxg4 37 hxg4 ♖xa7 38 ♕xa7 f4
39 ♗xf4!**

White sacrifices a piece back in order to begin a decisive attack on the black king.

**39...exf4 40 ♘h4! ♗f7**

40...♘f8 41 ♕d4+ ♔e6 42 ♘xg6 ♘xg6 43 ♗f5+ ♔f7 44 ♗xg6+ ♔xg6 45 ♕xd5 (Chandler) is winning for White. Material is level, but Black's king is too exposed for any hope of survival.

**41 ♕d4+ ♔e6**

41...♔g5 42 ♕g7 is decisive, for example 42...♕g8 43 ♘hf3+ ♔xg4 44 ♕h6 and ♘h2 mate, or 42...♔xh4 43 ♕h6+ ♔xg4 44 f3+ ♔g3 45 ♕h2 mate.

**42 ♘f5!**

The final tactic. Now Black's position falls apart.

**42...♗f8 43 ♕xf4 ♔d7 44 ♘d4 ♕e1+ 45 ♔g2 ♗d5+ 46 ♗e4 ♗xe4+ 47 ♘xe4 ♗e7 48 ♘xb5 ♘f8 49 ♘bxd6 ♘e6 50 ♕e5 1-0**

### Rook Lifts

On many occasions there are no open files on the board, but there are half-open files instead. These are files which are open to one side, but closed to the other. We will be studying many cases of

this in the future, especially in the section on pawns, but here I would like to give two examples, both from personal experience, where White uses a half-open file to transfer a rook along a rank. This is often referred to as a rook lift.

**Sadler-Emms**
British Ch. play-off (rapid), Hove 1997

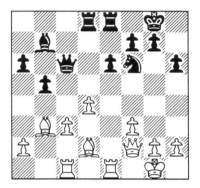

A quick glance at the position reveals that White has two half-open files (the b- and e-files) and Black has two also (the c- and d-files). Notice that White's rook on e1 and Black's rook on d8 are well placed, adding pressure along the half-open files.

Here I was reasonably happy with my position. Black's pieces are reasonably placed and White's isolated pawn couple (see page 73) is well restrained and may become weak later on. I thought that White's only real plus point was the pair of bishops, but Black's knight also has a reasonable outpost on d5. Sadler, however, using ranks and files, now showed excellent understanding of White's chances in this position.

**21 ♖e5!**

Exploiting the fifth rank. White may choose to double on the e-file with

♖ce1, or to occupy the outpost on c5. I decided that I should immediately ask the question of the rook.

**21...♘d7 22 ♖h5! ♘f6 23 ♖h3!**

In just three moves White has managed to manoeuvre his rook from e1 to h3 and suddenly Black has big problems defending on the kingside. White's idea is to play ♕h4 followed by crashing through with ♗xh6. I now felt that I had to do something drastic to stay in the game.

**23...e5**

Trying to open up the centre for my rooks. If White's attack fails then the rook on h3 will ultimately be useless in a battle on the central files. Unfortunately, the flip-side of this move is that White's bishop on b3 also comes to life, and the attack doesn't fail!

**24 ♗xh6! gxh6 25 ♖xh6 ♘g4?**

Black's only chance of survival lies with 25...♔f8 26 ♕h4 ♖xd4! 27 ♕xf6 ♕xf6 28 ♖xf6 ♖d7, although White has a good extra pawn on h2.

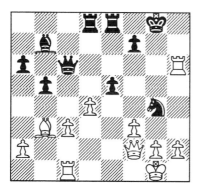

**26 ♖xc6?**

26 ♗xf7+! would have been immediately decisive, for example 26...♔f8 (26...♔xf7 27 fxg4+ wins) 27 ♖xc6 ♘xf2 28 ♗xe8 ♘d3 29 ♖d1 ♗xc6 30 ♗xc6

and White is three pawns to the good. After 26 ♖xc6, Black can battle on.

**26...♘xf2 27 ♖c7 ♘h3+! 28 gxh3 ♗d5 29 ♗xd5 ♖xd5 30 ♖e1 ♖e6 31 ♖xe5 ♖exe5 32 dxe5 ♖xe5 33 ♔f2**

Despite being two pawns to the good, it's still quite difficult for White to win this position due to the crippled pawns on the kingside. In the event, both Sadler and I made mistakes, but I made final one and ended up losing.

Here is a further example of a rook lift.

**Morris-Emms**
London 1993

In this position my opponent made imaginative use of his rook on a1.

**26 ♖a5!**

The rook controls the only 'open' rank on the board. But what is White planning to do?

**26...♗e7 27 ♖h5!**

This is the answer! White finds a very effective and aesthetically pleasing way of transporting his rook to the kingside, where it can take part in an assault against the black king.

**27...♗f8 28 ♖h3**

Now White has ideas of g4-g5, so I though my only chance was to block things up on the kingside.

**28...e5 29 f5! f6 30 ≌g3! ≗e7 31 h4**

and White is ready to crash through on the kingside with g4-g5. White has a winning advantage now, but my opponent misplayed his position later on and I managed to escape with a draw.

**Bishops and Diagonals**

We all know that bishops enjoy open spaces and long diagonals. They also work very well in pairs – one controls all the light squares whiles its partner controls all the dark squares. We shall study the power of the bishop pair a little later on, but for the moment I'd like to concentrate on the importance of diagonals.

**Exploiting Opening Diagonals**

The battle for an open diagonal can be just as important as a battle for an open file, especially in the opening and middlegame, when bishops can be just as effective as rooks. Once a diagonal is controlled, it usually favours the possessor if he can then 'lengthen the diagonal' and thus increase the scope of the attack-

ing bishop down that diagonal. It's instructive to see how Judit Polgar and Alexander Onischuk achieve this in the following examples.

**Hracek-J.Polgar**
Istanbul Olympiad 2000
*Sicilian Defence*

**1 e4 c5 2 ♘f3 e6 3 d4 cxd4 4 ♘xd4 ♘c6 5 ♘c3 ♕c7 6 ♗e3 a6 7 ♗d3 b5**

Judit Polgar enjoys playing this variation of the Taimanov Sicilian, which involves an early development of the c8-bishop along the long diagonal.

**8 ♘xc6 ♕xc6 9 0-0 ♗b7 10 a3**

Preventing any ideas of an early ...b5-b4. Another Polgar game continued 10 ♖e1 ♘e7!? 11 a4 b4 12 ♘a2 ♘g6 13 ♗d2 ♕b6 14 a5 ♕xa5 15 ♘xb4 ♕b6 16 ♘a2 ♗d6 17 ♕h5 ♗e5 and Black was at least equal, Macieja-J.Polgar, European Team Championship, Batumi 1999.

**10...♘f6 11 ♕e2**

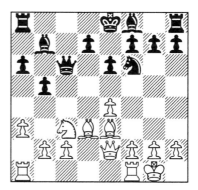

**11...h5!?**

This is a very ambitious move that aims to fight for control of the long g1-a7 diagonal, which currently in White's possession. More restrained ideas for Black include 11...♖c8 and 11...♗e7.

**12 f4?!**

This move is normally an integral part of White's expansion plans on the kingside, but here it's just a little too accommodating. White should have really taken the threat of ...♘g4 more seriously with either 12 h3 or 12 f3.

**12...♘g4!**

Polgar needs no second invitation.

**13 ♗d2 ♗c5+**

Black takes over an important diagonal, with a tempo gain to boot.

**14 ♔h1 ♗d4 15 ♖ae1 0-0-0!**

Queenside castling involves a certain amount of risk here, not least because the black king has only a little bit of pawn cover, but Polgar correctly assesses that she will be able to generate sufficient counterplay on the kingside. In any case, castling kingside would have made Black's previously play look a bit silly, not to mention that 15...0-0? 16 h3 ♘f6 17 e5 ♘d5 18 ♕xh5 is virtually winning for White.

**16 ♘d1?!**

After this passive move, Polgar takes over the operation. Ribli prefers the more aggressive 16 a4 b4 17 ♘a2.

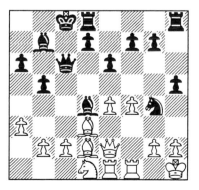

**16...f5!**

A crucial move, striving to increase

the scope of the bishop and queen along the a8-h1 diagonal (Black wishes to lengthen the diagonal). On the other hand, 16...d5?! 17 e5! would leave the bishop on b7 out of the game.

**17 ♗a5**

Ribli gives the line 17 exf5 exf5 (preparing ...♖he8) 18 ♗xf5 ♖he8 19 ♕f3 ♕xf3 20 gxf3 ♖xe1 21 ♗xe1 ♖f8 22 ♗e4 ♖xf4 23 ♗xb7+ ♔xb7 24 ♔g2 ♘e5 25 ♗g3 ♖f5 with an edge to Black.

**17...♖df8 18 c3 ♗a7**

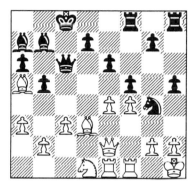

**19 e5?**

With this move White blocks the centre and kills off any chance of play on the e-file. Now Polgar can virtually do as she pleases on the kingside. Note how the black bishops and queen point menacingly along the long diagonals, like cruise missiles, towards the white king.

19 exf5! exf5 20 ♗b4 ♖f6 21 ♕c2 would at least gives White some chances to create some threats.

**19...g5!**

Polgar seizes her chance.

**20 c4**

White finally tries to open up the queenside, but it's a case of 'too little, too late'. 20 fxg5? ♘xe5 was the idea behind Polgar's last move – the knight cannot be captured due to the mate threat on g2. After 21 ♗c2 h4! 22 h3 ♖fg8 White has no good defence to Black simply capturing on g5 and piling up the pressure on the g2-pawn.

**20...bxc4 21 ♗xc4 gxf4 22 ♖f3**

Or 22 ♖xf4 ♖fg8!, and ...♘xe5 follows.

**22...♖hg8 23 b4**

23 ♗c3 h4 24 h3 ♘e3 25 ♘xe3 fxe3 keeps Black's iron-like grip on the game, for example 26 ♗b4 ♖xg2! 27 ♕xg2 ♕xf3 28 ♕xf3 ♗xf3+ 29 ♔h2 ♖g8 30 ♗xa6+ ♔d8 31 ♗a5+ ♔e8 32 ♗f1 e2! and Black wins.

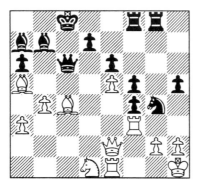

**23...♘xe5!**

With the capture of this pawn, White's position collapses.

**24 ♕xe5 ♕xc4 25 ♘b2 ♗xf3!**

A simple tactic to win the game. 26 ♘xc4 allows ...♗xg2 mate.

**26 gxf3 ♕c2 0-1**

There is no good defence to ...♕g2 mate. An impressive game by Polgar.

**Onischuk-Adianto**
Beijing 2000
*English Opening*

**1 c4 e5 2 ♘c3 ♗b4 3 ♕c2**

A rather early queen move, but as well as defending the knight on c3, the queen points along the long b1-h7 diagonal. This can useful for White as the queen can be utilised from long distance in an attack against Black's kingside.

**3...♘f6 4 ♘f3 ♘c6 5 ♘d5**

A typical move in this line of the English. White grabs the d5-square and prevents Black from opening up with ...d7-d5.

**5...a5**

Preparing to answer ♘xb4 with ...axb4, after which Black will have a half-open a-file at his disposal.

5...♘xd5? 6 cxd5 ♘d4 7 ♘xd4 exd4 simply loses a pawn after 8 ♕c4 or 8 ♕e4+.

**6 g3**

Preparing to fianchetto the bishop. 6 e3 followed by ♗d3, adding pressure to h7, is the alternative way to develop the kingside.

**6...0-0 7 ♗g2 d6 8 0-0 ♖e8**

With the e-pawn protected by ...d7-d6, 8...♘xd5 is now possible, although White keeps an edge after 9 cxd5 ♘e7 10 d4!.

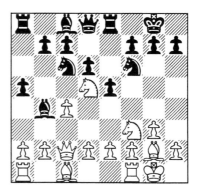

**9 ♘g5!**

By directly threatening h7, Onischuk force his opponent to make a slight weakness in his kingside pawn structure. At the moment this looks insignificant but White's dark-squared bishop has yet to come to life.

**9...g6 10 ♘xf6+ ♕xf6 11 ♘e4 ♕e7 12 d3**

Already Black is starting to feel the dark square problems on the kingside. White's initial threat is ♗g5.

**12...♘d4 13 ♕d1 ♘e6**

This relocation of the knight protects the g5-square.

**14 a3**

With this move White acquires the bishop pair as an advantage. If only Black could transplant this bishop back to g7 – all of his worries would be over.

**14...♗c5 15 ♘xc5 dxc5?!**

I agree with Ribli that Black should have opted for the simpler 15...♘xc5, with the idea of clamping down on the queenside with ...a5-a4. Then 16 b3 a4 (or 16...e4 – Ribli) gives Black more chances of counterplay.

**16 b3!**

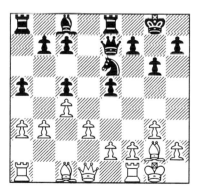

Simply preparing to fianchetto the dark-squared bishop onto a very good diagonal. With Black's d6-pawn gone, the e5-pawn now lacks natural protection. The advance ...f7-f6 will eventually be forced but this will weaken Black's kingside even further.

**16...♖a6!**

Preparing to hit the b3-pawn with ...♖b6.

**17 ♗b2 ♕d6 18 e3!?**

A brave decision. Onischuk wants to keep the black knight out of the d4-square forever, although after this move Black gets a certain amount of counterplay against both b3 and d3.

**18...♖d8 19 ♕c1 ♖b6?**

Adianto misses his chance to complicate. Ribli gives the line 19...♕xd3!? 20 ♗xe5 ♖b6 with counterplay for Black, despite the fact that White has total control over the long a1-h8 diagonal. If White then continues with 21 ♗d5?, Black can hit back with 21...♖xd5! 22 cxd5 ♕xd5, and with threats of ...♘g5 it's suddenly White who has all the problems on the *light* squares!

**20 ♕c3! f6**

If 20...♕xd3? 21 ♕xe5! and Black is killed down the long diagonal.

**21 ♖ad1**

Now White has a clear advantage. All of Black's threats against b3 and d3 have been neutralised and White can prepare to chip away at the a1-h8 diagonal with a timely f2-f4.

**21...♘g7 22 f4!**

Why wait?

**22...♗g4?!**

This allows a winning combination. Black has to go in for 22...exf4 although after 23 ♖xf4 ♘f5 24 ♗d5+! ♔g7 25 ♖df1 I don't fancy his survival chances, such is White's pressure along the diagonals and the half-open f-file.

**23 ♗d5+ ♔h8 24 fxe5 fxe5 25 ♕xe5!**

The diagonal is cleared of wood and White's threats are immediately decisive.

**25...♛xe5 26 ♝xe5 ♝xd1 27 ♝xc7**

Despite being temporarily a rook up, Black has no way out.

**27...♝e2**

27...♜bd6 28 ♝xd6 ♜xd6 allows mate in one with 29 ♖f8.

**28 ♝xd8 ♝xf1 29 ♝xb6 ♝xd3 30 ♝xc5 1-0**

White has two extra pawns and is winning more.

### Relocating to Better Diagonals

Sometimes a great diagonal can suddenly become available, but the bishop required to fill the diagonal is currently languishing somewhere else. On this occasion it can be a very useful positional manoeuvre to relocate the bishop to that desirable diagonal. In many circumstances the dynamics of the position make this impossible, but in quiet, manoeuvring positions, like the one below, this relocation can prove to be decisive.

### Emms-Belov
German Bundesliga 1995

White's plus points in this position include the backward d6-pawn, outposts on b5 and d5, and good control of the light squares. But how can White's overall advantage be increased? Well, every piece is well positioned except for the bishop on f3, whose influence on the game is minimal due to being blocked by the e4-pawn. In a quiet position like this White can simply take time out to improve the position of his worst piece, relocating it to a much more favourable diagonal.

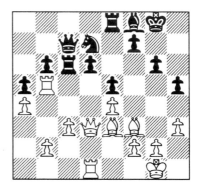

**21 ♝e2! ♞c5?**

It seems very natural to attack the white queen, but this falls in with White's plans. 21...♝e7 is stronger, although even after this White can eventually activate his bishop on the f1-a6 diagonal: 22 ♛c2 ♜b8 23 ♜b3 ♞c5 24 ♜a3 ♛d8 25 ♝b5 ♜cc8 26 ♜aa1 and White will continue by doubling on the d-file.

**22 ♛c2 ♜b8**

Or 22...♞e6 23 ♜bd5! and the bishop is coming to b5.

**23 ♝c4! ♛e7 24 ♝d5**

In just a few moves the bishop has been transformed from being a 'big pawn' on f3 into a piece with great influence on the game; White's advantage is now much more pronounced.

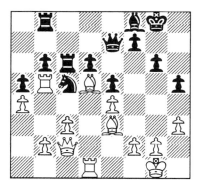

**24...♖c7?**

24...♖cc8 is more resilient

**25 b4! axb4 26 cxb4 ♘e6 27 ♕d2 ♖bc8 28 ♗xe6 fxe6 29 ♖xb6**

and I went on to win relatively easily.

**Vacating Diagonals**

So what do you do if your opponent has control over a long and important diagonal? One possibility is to fight for control by placing your bishop on the same diagonal. However, this may either be impossible or impractical.

Another defensive procedure involves simply moving all your pieces off the diagonal, with the result that the opposing bishop looks impressive, but actually just hits 'thin air'.

**Spiridonov-Chuchelov**

French League 2000

*English Opening*

**1 ♘f3 ♘f6 2 c4 c5 3 g3 d5 4 cxd5 ♘xd5 5 ♘c3 ♘c6 6 ♘xd5 ♕xd5 7 ♗g2 e5 8 d3 ♗e7 9 0-0 0-0 10 ♗e3**

Black's pawns on c5 and e5 (the so-called Maroczy Bind) give him a pleasant space advantage, but White is well developed and his last move threatens to de-stroy Black's queenside structure with ♘d4. Watch how Black effectively clears the h1-a8 diagonal.

**10...♕e6!**

Preventing White's threat.

**11 ♘d2**

Or 11 ♕b3!? and now:

a) 11...♕xb3 12 axb3 gives White doubled b-pawns, but the half-open a-file is useful, for example 12...♗d7 13 ♖fc1 b6 14 b4! cxb4 15 d4! with a small but useful initiative.

b) 11...♖b8! (Black continues to vacate) 12 ♖fc1 b6 13 ♕xe6 ♗xe6 14 ♘g5 ♗xg5 15 ♗xg5 ♘d4 16 ♔f1 f6 17 ♗d2 a5! and Black is fine, Andersson-Timman, Tilburg 1987 – the bishop on g2 simply stares into a vacuum.

**11...♖b8!**

A second piece is removed from the diagonal. Black prepares to support his c-pawn with ...b7-b6.

**12 ♘e4 b6 13 f4**

If White doesn't strike back, then Black will catch up in development and retain a space advantage.

**13...f5 14 ♘c3 ♔h8!**

Vacating another diagonal (a2-g8). Now ♗d5 is no longer a worry.

**15 ♕a4**

**15...&d7!?**

In his notes in *ChessBase Magazine* Chuchelov gives the worthwhile alternative 15...&b7!? 16 &d5 ₩d6 17 &xc6 &xc6 18 fxe5 (18 ₩xa7? loses after 18...Ia8 19 ₩xb6 Ifb8 20 fxe5 ₩e6 21 ₩c7 Ib7 and the queen is trapped) 18...₩xe5 19 &f4 ₩e6 20 ₩xa7 Ib7 21 ₩a6 &f6 22 Iae1 g5 23 &d2 f4, after which Black has excellent play for the pawn disadvantage. Note that in this variation the long h1-a8 diagonal is now firmly in Black's possession!

**16 fxe5 &xe5 17 &d5!**

17 ₩xa7? loses to 17...&c6 18 &xc6 ₩xe3+ 19 If2 &xc6.

**17...₩d6!**

17...&xa4 18 &xe6 &d7 19 &xd7 &xd7 is equal, but Black plays for more.

**18 ₩d1?!**

Black is dictating events so White may as well be a pawn up for his troubles. After 18 ₩xa7 Chuchelov gives 18...b5 19 &g2 (19 &f4 b4 20 &xe5 ₩xe5 21 ₩xd7 bxc3 22 ₩e6 ₩xe6 23 &xe6 cxb2 24 Iab1 g6 is very good for Black) 19...&c6! 20 &xc6 &xc6 21 ₩a6 ₩d7 22 &f4 b4 23 &d1 Ia8 24 ₩c4 &d4 25 If2 &f6! and Black is very active, but at least White still has that extra pawn.

**18...&f6**

Black has removed all his pieces from the h1-a8 diagonal and the bishop on d5 is rather less effective. Black is clearly better now – his position is more compact and White may have problems defending down the central files.

**19 &f4 g5! 20 &xe5 &xe5 21 &g2 &d4+ 22 &h1 f4! 23 gxf4 gxf4 24 ₩e1 Ibe8**

Now White has problems with his weak e2-pawn.

**25 Ic1 ₩h6!**

Intending to play ...Ig8 and ...&h3. White's in big trouble now, but his next move, influenced by time-trouble, makes sure that the end is quick.

**26 &d1?? f3!**

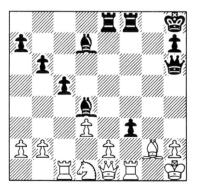

The rook on c1 is hanging.

**27 ♖xf3 ♖xf3 0-1**

**Marin-Golubev**
Bucharest 1996
*King's Indian Defence*

**1 ♘f3 ♘f6 2 g3 g6 3 ♗g2 ♗g7 4 0-0 0-0 5 c4 d6 6 d4 ♘bd7 7 ♘c3 e5 8 e4 a6 9 h3 exd4 10 ♘xd4 ♖e8 11 ♖e1**

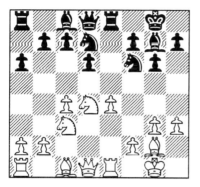

We've reached a fairly typical position from the Fianchetto Variation of the King's Indian Defence. Both Black's and White's next moves are 'vacating the diagonal'.

**11...♖b8**

Black plans to create counterplay on the queenside with ...c7-c5 followed by ...b7-b5. Thus the rook is nudged to b8, where it is conveniently out of the firing line from the g2-bishop.

**12 ♖b1**

White follows a similar prophylactic path, taking measures along the long a1-h8 diagonal before the problems arise. Following 12 b3 Black reacts with 12...c5 13 ♘c2 b5!, for example 14 cxb5 (14 ♕xd6 ♖b6 15 ♕d1 b4 16 ♘d5! ♘xd5 17 cxd5 {Knaak} is interesting – White

sacrifices the exchange on a1, but has two powerful pawns in the centre, plus some dark square control) 14...axb5 15 ♕xd6 ♖b6 16 ♕d1 b4 17 ♘a4 ♖be6 18 ♗b2 ♕e7 19 ♘e3 ♗b7 20 f3 ♘h5 21 ♗xg7 ♔xg7 22 g4 ♘f4 23 ♕d2 ♘e5 and Black has strong pressure for the pawn, Whiteley-Gallagher, Royan 1989.

**12...♘e5 13 b3 c5 14 ♘c2**

Now White is left with only one piece on the a1-h8 diagonal, and so Black's influence along this diagonal is less important.

**14...♘h5!? 15 ♘e3**

This was awarded two exclamation marks by Marin and Golubev, but is this really deserved? After 15 ♗b2?! f5! 16 f4 ♘c6 17 exf5 ♗xf5, Black's bishops give him tremendous counterplay. White should consider vacating the diagonal completely with 15 ♘e2, when I think White is slightly better.

**15...b5?**

In *Informator* Marin and Golubev give the long line 15...♘xc4! (it's my exclamation mark) 16 ♘xc4 ♗xc3 17 ♖e2 ♗d4 18 ♗e3 b5 19 ♗xd4 cxd4 20 ♘a3!? ♕a5 21 ♘c2 ♕xa2 22 ♘b4 ♕a3 23 ♕xd4 a5 24 ♘c6 ♖b7 25 b4! axb4 26 ♘xb4 and White has very good pressure for the pawn deficit. However, 17...b5! looks good for Black, as 18 ♘xd6 ♖e6 19 ♕c2 ♗d4 20 ♘xc8 ♘xg3! 21 ♖e3 ♘h5 22 ♘a7 ♕d7 will leave Black a pawn up with a good position.

**16 cxb5 axb5 17 ♗b2 b4 18 ♘cd5 ♗a6 19 ♕d2!**

Now in the game Golubev played 19...♘f6 and after 20 ♘xf6+ ♗xf6 21 ♘d5 ♗g7 22 ♖bd1 White was slightly better, going on to win a long endgame. In the notes, however, the players give

the enticing

**19...♘d3 20 ♗xg7! ♘xe1 21 ♗a1 ♘xg2 22 ♔xg2!**

when Black is the exchange to the good, but White has absolute control over the long a1-h8 diagonal. This proves to be the most significant fact. Their analysis runs:

**22...♗b7**

Or 22...♖xe4 23 g4 ♖e2 24 ♕h6 ♕f8 25 ♕xf8+ ♔xf8 26 gxh5 ♖xa2 27 ♘f6 ♔e7 28 h6 with a clear advantage.

**23 ♘gf4! ♘xf4**

Alternatively:

a) 23...♕g5 24 ♕b2 ♖e5 (or 24...♕e5 25 ♕c2!) 25 h4 ♕d8 26 ♘xh5 gxh5 27

f4 and White wins

b) 23...♗xd5 24 ♘xh5 gxh5 25 ♕h6 f6 26 ♗xf6 ♕d7 27 ♕g5+ ♔f8 28 ♕xd5 and Black's kingside is destroyed.

**24 ♘f6+ ♕xf6**

Or 24...♔f8 25 ♘xh7+ ♔g8 26 ♘f6+ ♔f8 27 ♕xf4 and White's attack is worth much more than the insignificant material disadvantage.

**25 ♗xf6 ♘h5**

25...♘xh3+ 26 ♔h2 ♖e6 27 ♗a1 ♗xe4 28 ♖e1! and ♕h6 is a big threat.

**26 ♕xd6 ♘xf6 27 ♕xf6 ♗xe4 28 ♖e1 ♗d5 29 ♖xe8+ ♖xe8 30 g4! ♗e6 31 f3 ♖c8 32 h4**

and White has good winning chances.

# CHAPTER THREE

# The Bishop Pair

As I've already stated, bishops work very well in pairs. As they control different coloured squares, one piece complements the other and together they can be a powerful force. In this chapter I would like to study how well they compare to the 'bishop and knight pair'.

### Some Statistics

It's commonly known that, in general, the bishop pair slightly outweighs the 'bishop and knight pair'. I was, however, quite keen to find out the statistics in practical play. So using *Mega Database 2001* (a chess database with over 1,600,000 good quality games) and some functions of the chess database program *ChessBase*, I managed to come up with some answers, some of which are shown below.

### Test 1

Here I checked for positions where each side possessed no queens, 0-2 rooks (i.e. the number of rooks was irrelevant) and two minor pieces each (one side had two bishops while the other side had bishop and knight). Basically I was checking how well the bishop pair fared against the bishop and knight in endgame situations. To ensure a reasonably stable position I added the proviso that this situation lasted for at least 20 half moves (ten moves from either side). The results were as follows:

### Results

**White has bishop pair** (17161 games)
White scores 65%
Average white rating: 2352
Average black rating: 2322

**Black has bishop pair** (16367 games)
Black scores 61 %
Average white rating: 2305
Average black rating: 2338

### Conclusions

At master level, on average White scores 54% (Black scores 46%). So we can easily see that the bishop pair influences the result very much in a positive way, with

White scoring 11% more than usual and Black scoring a massive 15% more. Some of this can be explained by the fact that the possessor of the bishop pair was on average just over 30 Elo rating points higher the possessor of the bishop and knight, but using expected score ratios this only affects results by about 5%. Thus, even taking this into consideration, the two bishops still score very well. Going back to the rating differences, this shows that higher rated players either appreciate the bishop pair more, or are using their strength to force their opponents in to giving up the bishop pair!

## Test 2

The conditions for this test were the following:

Both sides possessed a queen, two rooks and a knight. One side also possessed a bishop pair, while the other possessed a further bishop and knight. Once again there was a proviso of 20 half-moves. On this occasion I wanted to check how well both White and Black had scored after a relatively early exchange of bishop for knight, most likely in the opening stages of a game.

## Results

White has bishop pair (61930 games)
White scores 59%
Average white rating: 2352
Average black rating: 2338

Black has bishop pair (58360 games)
Black scores 51%
Average white rating: 2327
Average black rating: 2334

## Conclusions

Both White and Black again score better with the bishop pair, but this time only 5% better than normal, and this trims down to 3% when average ratings are taken into consideration.

This concurs with the fact that when a side gives up a bishop for a knight in the opening or early middlegame, often there is a compensatory factor, which could be either structural, developmental or both. Common examples of this are in the Ruy Lopez Exchange Variation and the Nimzo Indian Defence.

## Exploiting Open Spaces with the Bishop Pair

### H.Hunt-Emms
Vera Menchik Mem., Maidstone 1994

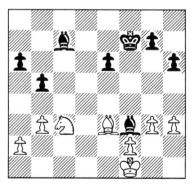

We begin with a look at an open position in an endgame, where the bishops really do rule the roost. It certainly helps Black that there are pawns on both sides of the board – White will be stretched trying to defend against the long-range power of the bishop pair. Another point in Black's favour in this particular position is his authority of the light squares, emphasised by the dominant bishop on f3.

There is one piece of good news for White – Black's isolated e-pawn is a weakness, not so much in that it can be attacked, but more that White's bishop has a useful defensive outpost on e3. Black would have stronger winning chances with an f-pawn instead of an e-pawn.

During the game I felt my advantages should add up to a win, although looking at the position now I couldn't confidently assess the position as 'winning for Black'. What I can definitely say is that White has a long arduous defensive task ahead.

**46 ♔e1?!**

I suspect that 46 h4! is more resilient, after which Black has no obvious target. Following the text Black is able to target the h-pawn.

**46...g5!**

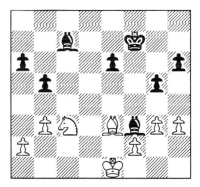

Now Black wants to play ...♗g2 and force the pawn to h4. After an exchange on h4 White's h-pawn will be extremely vulnerable.

**47 ♔d2 ♔g6 48 ♘e2 e5 49 ♘c3?**

49 ♘g1!? looks incredibly passive, but it's White's best chance of a successful defence: 49...♗c6 50 ♗c5 h5 51 ♔e3

and now 51...h4? is premature – 52 gxh4 gxh4 53 ♗e7 ♔h5 54 ♘f3 ♗d7 55 ♘xh4 ♗xh3 and the simplification of the pawns on the kingside should ensure that White draws. This is a case of White just 'hanging on in there' and punishing impatient play.

**49...♗g2**

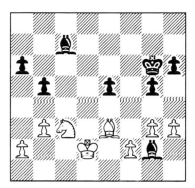

Now the h-pawn is lost and the winning process is reasonably straightforward.

**50 h4 gxh4 51 gxh4 ♗d8 52 f4 exf4 53 ♗xf4 ♗xh4 54 ♔d3 ♗f6 55 a4 h5 56 axb5 axb5 57 ♘e4**

57 ♘xb5 loses to the skewer 57...♗f1+.

**57...♗e7 58 ♘d6 h4 59 ♔d4 ♗c6 60 ♔c5 ♗d7 61 ♔b6 ♗xd6**

The simplest. On this occasion the notoriously drawish opposite-coloured bishop ending is winning for Black – soon it will be only a single bishop ending with Black having the bishop!

**62 ♗xd6 ♔h5 63 ♔c7 ♗e8 64 ♔d8 ♗f7 65 b4 ♔g4 66 ♔e7 ♗c4 67 ♔f6 h3**

Black will play ...♔f3-g2 and ...h3-h2.

**Opening Lines for the Bishop Pair**

With all other things being equal (for

example, development and space etc.), it's usually beneficial for the player with the bishop pair to open the position up, thus giving him a chance to exploit their long-range power. Exceptions occur (and they do quite often) when the side with the bishop pair is lagging behind in development. On these occasions the possessor of the bishop pair will only try open the position after regrouping or catching up in development.

### Giddins-Emms
### Isle of Man 1999

Here is a crucial early middlegame position. It's true that Black has the bishop pair, but at the moment both are blocked by pawns and neither is influencing the game. It could be said that the position is 'semi-open', that is, there is definite potential for the position to open up. The trick for Black is to open it to *his* advantage.

Both sides have pawn weaknesses – White has an isolated d-pawn while Black has weaknesses on c6 and e6. Black could unleash his dark-squared bishop with ...f6-f5, but this would be a grave positional concession, leaving White with a nice juicy outpost on e5.

Black could also consider ...e6-e5, but after an exchange on e5, Black would be left with a terrible pawn structure – four pawn islands in all (see page 62).

Instead Black's aim should be to liberate the bishop on b7 with ...c7-c5!. Indeed, the battle around this advance is the key to whole position.

**18...♖ac8**

Preparing ...c7-c5, which White prevents with his next move.

**19 ♖c3 ♗f8!**

Again threatening ...c7-c5; this time White has no good way of stopping the advance, as 20 ♖c1 leaves the a2-pawn hanging.

**20 a3 c5!**

Just in time. Any delay would have been met with ♖c1, when White would have the advantage.

**21 dxc5 ♖xc5 22 ♖xc5 ♕xc5 23 ♕xc5 ♗xc5**

The situation has clarified and it's now much easier to see that Black is in command. The position has been opened and there are pawns on both sides of the board – just the sort of situation in which the long-range power of the bishop pair come into its own.

**24 ♖c1 ♖c8**

Incidentally threatening 25...♗xf2+.

**25 ♗f4 ♔f7 26 b4 ♗f8 27 ♖xc8 ♗xc8**

The exchange of rooks has not hindered Black's progress. Notice that the black king can try and penetrate on the light squares, on which White has little control. On the other hand, the progress of the white king will be severely hampered by black's annoying bishops.

**28 ♘d2 e5 29 ♗e3 a6 30 ♔f1 ♔e6**

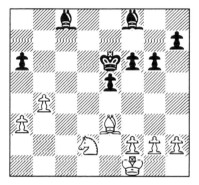

**31 f4?**

My opponent tries to exchange pawns, which is only natural (exchange all of them and a draw is secured!). However, this particular exchange only helps to open the position even further, thus giving the bishop pair more scope.

White should really be trying to bring his king into the centre, for example 31 ♔e2 ♔d5 32 f3, followed by ♔d3, would have made my task much more difficult.

**31...exf4 32 ♗xf4 ♔d5**

Now my king is ready to infiltrate with ...♔d4-c3.

**33 ♗e3?**

Preventing ...♔d4, but now Black has the extra idea of ...♗d6-e5-b2, a consequence of White's 31st move.

The more resilient 33 ♔e2 is proposed by the Hungarian grandmaster Zoltan Ribli in *ChessBase Magazine*. If 33...♔d4 then 34 ♗e3+! ♔c3 35 ♘e4+ ♔b2 36 ♘xf6 ♔xa3 37 ♗c5 gives White more hope of hanging on.

**33...♗d7 34 ♔e2 ♗d6! 35 h3 ♗b5+ 36 ♔f3 ♗e5**

Now the simple threat of ...♗b2 is too much for White.

**37 ♘e4**

Or 37 ♘b3 ♗b2 38 ♗c1 ♗xc1 39 ♘xc1 ♔c4 40 ♔e3 ♔c3 and White can do nothing against the threat of ...♔b2, winning the queenside pawns.

**37...♗b2 38 ♗d2 f5 39 ♘c3+**

Or 39 ♘g5 h5 and the b-pawn is a goner.

**39...♔c4**

There was still time for me mess things up: 39...♗xc3?? 40 ♗xc3 ♔c4 41 ♗e5 ♔b3 42 ♗d6 ♔xa3 43 ♔f2 leaves Black a pawn up, but with no chance of making any further progress due to the opposite-coloured bishops.

**40 ♘xb5 axb5**

White has eliminated one of Black's bishops but it's too late. Black will clean up the queenside pawns.

**41 g4 fxg4+ 42 ♔xg4 ♗xa3 43 ♔g5**

♗xb4 44 ♗f4 ♗f8 45 ♔f6 b4 46 ♔f7 b3 47 ♗e5

Or 47 ♗c1 ♗b4 48 ♔g8 ♔d3 49 ♗b2 ♔c2 50 ♗f6 ♗c3 and the b-pawn promotes.

**47...♗b4 0-1**

Black wins after 48 ♗b2 ♔d3 49 ♔g8 ♔c2 50 ♗e5 ♗c3.

**Gradual Exploitation of the Bishop Pair**
Long term exploitation of the bishop pair is an important technique which is difficult to master and often only comes after much practice and experience.

I found the following example to be very enlightening. It's interesting to see how Sergei Dolmatov, a renowned technician, improves his position bit by bit, using his bishop pair to force small concessions by his opponent.

### Dolmatov-Burmakin
Elista 2001

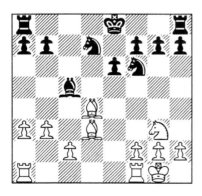

Black has just played ...♗c5, offering the exchange of dark-squared bishops. What should White do?

**16 ♗b2!**

To the untrained eye this might seem like a loss of tempo and a step backwards, but to keep any small advantage,

it's crucial that White retains the bishop pair. With an open position and pawns on both sides of the board, the long range power of the bishops will once again outweigh the bishop and knight pair. Another point to bear in mind is that White can use the vulnerability of the bishop on c5 to galvanise his queen-side pawn majority.

On the other hand, 16 ♗xc5?! would be an instructive error and would even leave White facing potential problems regarding dark square control. After 16...♘xc5 17 ♗b5+ ♔e7 Black will follow up with ...♖hd8. Notice that 18 b4?! ♘ce4 19 ♘xe4 ♘xe4 20 ♖fd1 ♖hd8 leaves White having to deal with the awkward threat of ...♘c3.

**16...0-0-0 17 b4 ♗b6**

Black can also try 17...♗d6 with the positional idea of ...♗e5, once again offering the exchange of bishops. In turn, White should prevent this act with 18 ♖fe1, following up with ♖ad1 and c2-c4.

**18 ♖ad1**

Sensibly bringing a rook to the centre.

**18...♘b8 19 ♗e2 ♖xd1 20 ♖xd1 ♘bd7?!**

Annotating this game for *ChessBase Magazine*, the Israeli Grandmaster Alexander Finkel criticised this move, preferring Black to offer another exchange of rooks with 20...♖d8. He gives the line 21 ♖xd8+ ♔xd8 22 ♗f3 ♘c6 23 c4 ♗c7 24 ♔f1 ♗e5 25 ♗c1! (keeping the bishop pair – after 25 ♗xe5?! ♘xe5 26 ♗xb7 ♘xc4 27 a4 ♔c7 White is losing control) and assesses the position as slightly better for White.

**21 c4 ♗c7 22 ♗d4 a6 23 ♘h5! ♘xh5?!**

Again Finkel was unimpressed by

Black's play, suggesting instead the calm 23...♖g8. After the text Black will be forced to play...e6-e5, which will weaken his control over the light squares. This is particularly important as Black has no light-squared bishop to compensate for this.

**24 ♗xh5 e5**

After 24...f6 White can force...e6-e5 with 25 ♗f7.

**25 ♗c3 g6 26 ♗e2 ♖d8**

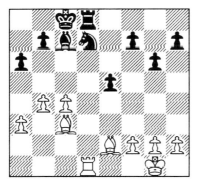

**27 c5**

Logical play. Black has no light-squared bishop to oppose White's so it's only natural that White should attack on the light squares with ♗c4.

**27...♘b8 28 ♖xd8+ ♔xd8 29 ♗c4 f6 30 f3 b6 31 cxb6 ♗xb6+ 32 ♔f1 ♗e3 33 ♗b2?!**

Finkel prefers the more direct 33 ♔e2 ♗c1 34 a4 ♔e7 35 ♔d3 ♔d6 36 ♗g8! h6 37 ♗h7 g5 38 ♔e4 and already Black is teetering on the brink, for example 38...♘c6 39 b5 axb5 40 axb5 ♘d4 41 ♗b4+ ♔d7 42 b6 ♔c6 43 ♗e7 ♔xb6 44 ♗xf6 and the bishops will clean up on the kingside.

**33...♔c7 34 ♔e2 ♗g1 35 h3 ♔b6 36 ♗g8!**

Forcing the pawns onto dark squares,

thus paving the way for the white king to enter via the light ones.

**36...h6 37 ♗f7 g5 38 ♔d3**

With the simple threat of ♔e4-f5.

**38...♘c6 39 ♔e4 ♗d4?!**

Of course, by now Dolmatov is used to sidestepping the offer to exchange bishops. Finkel prefers to put the knight on d4, for example 39...♘d4! 40 ♗c4 (40 ♔d5!?) 40...a5! (exchanging pawns in general eases Black's defence) 41 ♔d5 axb4 42 axb4 ♔c7 and it will be more difficult for White to crack Black's position.

**40 ♗c1!**

Naturally. Now the knight is forced to a passive square in order to prevent penetration with ♔f5.

**40...♘e7 41 g4 ♔b5 42 ♔d3 ♘c8**

42...♔a4? falls into a surprising mating net after 43 ♔c4! and ♗c8.

**43 ♗c4+ ♔b6 44 ♔e4**

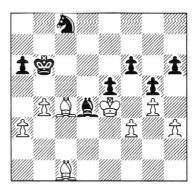

**44...♘e7**

Finally Black can exchange knight for bishop with 44...♘d6+ 45 ♔d5 ♘xc4 46 ♔xc4, but now we see the fruits of White's earlier work. All black's kingside pawns are on dark squares and can be eaten by white's remaining bishop: 46...♔c6 47 a4 ♗f2 48 b5+ axb5+ 49 axb5+ ♔b6 50 ♗a3, followed by ♗e7.

**45 ♗d2 ♔b7 46 a4 ♔b6 47 ♗f7 ♗f2 48 ♗c3 ♗g1?**

The final mistake. Black should keep his bishop on f2 in order to prevent what's coming.

**49 ♗e1!**

After this move the win is no longer in any doubt. Dolmatov plans to push the h-pawn to h5, after which any infiltration of king to g6 or bishop to f8 will be immediately decisive, given the advanced position of the h-pawn.

**49...♗d4 50 h4 ♔c6**

Black cannot play 50...gxh4 51 ♗xh4 as the f6-pawn will drop immediately.

**51 h5! ♔b6 52 ♗c4**

Now Dolmatov simply plans to relocate the dark-squared bishop to a3 and then push with b4-b5.

**52...♗g1**

There is no escape: 52...♗b2 loses to 53 ♗f2+ ♔b7 54 ♗c5.

**53 ♗c3 ♗f2 54 ♗b2! 1-0**

On first sight resignation seems a little premature, but there is nothing that Black can do to prevent White's winning plan, for example 54...♗e1 55 ♗a3 (threatening b4-b5) 55...♘c6 56 b5 axb5 57 axb5 ♗b4 (or 57...♘b4 58 ♗f1 and

♔f5-g6) 58 ♗xb4 ♘xb4 59 ♔f5 ♔c5 60 ♗f1 ♘d5 61 ♔g6. Great technique from the Russian Grandmaster.

**When Opening Lines is a Struggle**

Before we get too carried away thinking how brilliant the bishop pair is when compared to the 'bishop and knight pair' in semi-open positions, I should give a couple of examples to readdress the balance. In both of the following examples you could hardly call the position 'blocked'. There is certainly potential to open them up, but positional nuances present the player with the bishop pair with concrete problems.

**Morozevich-Piket**
Internet (rapidplay) 2000

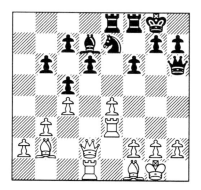

On first sight this position looks very favourable for White, who has the bishop pair and more space. However, to emphasise the strength of the bishops White will have to try and open the position up with f2-f4 and e4-e5. This will prove to be extremely difficult as Black's pieces are well placed to combat this idea. Indeed, playing f2-f4 too early may only end up leaving White with a vulnerable pawn on e4.

Note that, despite the doubled pawns, Black has a good solid pawn structure. The aesthetically pleasing diamond (c5, b6, c7, d6) is particularly strong – all the pawns protect each other except the base on c7, and this is virtually immune to attack. The bishop will fit snugly into c6, adding pressure to the e4-pawn.

**20 ♗c3 ♗c6 21 ♕b2 ♘g6 22 ♖de1 ♖e7**

Black's position is easy to play; he simply lines up his forces against the e4-pawn.

**23 ♗d2 ♕h5 24 ♗e2 ♕e5 25 ♗c3 ♕e6 26 ♗f1 ♖fe8 27 ♕d2 ♕f7**

Also possible is the more ambitious 27...♕c8!?, planning to play...♕a8!. Note, however, that although Black's position is extremely sound, he still does best by waiting patiently for White to over-extend. Black's only real pawn break is ...f6-f5, but he is loath to open up the position for White's bishop pair unless there is major positional compensation. If White starts throwing his kingside pawns forward, ...f6-f5 may be a good counterattacking stroke, but on its own it may just open the position to White's favour.

**28 f3 ♔f8**

**29 ♕f2**

More ambitious is 29 g3, planning ♗g2 and f3-f4, but this is not without risks, for example 29...♘e5 (29...♕e6 30 ♗g2 ♕c8 31 f4 ♕a8 is also possible – 32 ♕c2 f5! 33 e5 ♗xg2 34 ♕xg2 ♕xg2+ 35 ♔xg2 dxe5 36 fxe5 ♔f7 and ...♔e6 looks fine for Black) 30 ♗g2 f5!? 31 exf5 ♘xf3+ 32 ♗xf3 ♗xf3 33 ♖xe7 ♖xe7 34 ♖xe7 ♕xe7 and Black is no worse.

**29...♗b7 30 ♗d3**

Once again White can consider 30 g3!?, although after 30...♘e5 31 h3 ♔g8 32 ♗g2 ♕g6 33 f4 ♘d7 it's not clear how White makes any real progress without risk.

**30...♘f4 31 ♗c2 ♕g6**

Threatening ...♘h3+.

**32 ♕g3**

The Israeli grandmaster Viktor Mikhalevski points out that White's final chance to play for the advantage is with 32 ♔h1 as after the text move Black can prevent any useful kingside pawn advance.

**32...♕xg3 33 hxg3 ♘e6**

This knight may be threatening to hop into d4.

**34 ♖d1 ♘g5**

With every black piece pointing at

e4, White will find it virtually impossible to arrange f3-f4. Note that, as a result of the queen exchange on g3, White no longer has the possibility of h2-h4, so the g5 square is a useful outpost for the black knight.

**35 g4 h6 36 ♔f2 ♘e6 37 ♖ee1 ♔f7 38 ♖d2 ♘d8 39 ♗d3**

and the players agreed a draw. Some might say this game had 'grandmaster draw' written all over it, but in truth it's difficult for either side to do anything constructive without compromising his own position.

The next example of a semi-open position holds not many fears for the possessor of the bishop and knight pair.

**Nikolaev-Tunik**
St Petersburg 2000

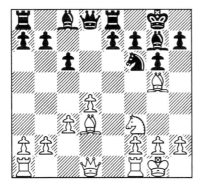

A typical position has arisen in which White's central pawn on d4 gives him slightly more space. Black, on the other hand, is extremely solid, and the exchange of one pair of minor pieces has helped to release some of the pressure.

**12...♗g4!**

At first sight this is quite surprising, as after h2-h3 Black is induced into giving up bishop for knight for no particular

compensation. Nevertheless, most grandmasters wouldn't hesitate before playing such a move. Black's idea is to deliberately exchange this bishop for the knight on f3. With two sets of minor pieces off the board, Black will not suffer from lack of space. It's true that White will possess the bishop pair but, due to the pawn structure and Black's remaining pieces, it will be very difficult for White to open up the position to his advantage. In my opinion Black is already close to reaching equality.

An example of Black suffering after refraining from this simplifying move is 12...♕b6 13 ♕d2! (now ...♗g4 can be met with ♘e5) 13...♗e6 14 ♖fe1 ♗d5 15 ♘e5 ♖ad8 16 b4 ♕c7 17 a4 ♗e6 18 ♗f4, Anilkumar-Barcenilla, Calcutta 1994 – White has a good knight on e5 and a handy space advantage.

**13 h3?!**

This only encourages Black to carry out his plan. Stronger is 13 ♗c4, moving the bishop onto a more prosperous diagonal and eliminating the possibility of ...♕d5.

**13...♗xf3 14 ♕xf3 ♕d5!**

Presenting White with an uncomfortable dilemma: White must choose between exchanging queens, after which any initiative he has is gone, or protecting his bishop, when the queen may be awkwardly placed.

**15 ♕xd5**

Following 15 ♕g3 Black can exchange knight for bishop with 15...♘e4 16 ♗xe4 ♕xe4, as 17 ♖ae1 is met by the infiltrating 17...♕c2!.

The only other move to protect the bishop is 15 ♕f4, but then 15...c5! threatens to lumber White with a vulnerable isolated d-pawn.

**15...♘xd5**

It's true that White has retained the bishop pair, but Black can be quite satisfied with his position. The knight on d5 is well placed, especially as any attempt to evict it with c3-c4 would leave White's d-pawn extremely vulnerable. As a consequence, it's very difficult for White to open the position to his advantage.

I should also point out that 15...cxd5 is also perfectly playable – Black has a rock-solid position. White should probably reply with 16 a4, preventing Black from beginning a minority attack with ...b7-b5 (see page 117).

**16 ♖fe1 e6 17 ♗h4?!**

It has to be said that White's play for the rest of this game is quite aimless, but this does give us a good chance to see how Black should play in an ideal world. I prefer the restraining 17 a4!, which would at least make Black think twice about expansion on the queenside.

**17...b5! 18 ♗g3**

Or 18 a4 b4! and White begins to feel the effects of the fianchettoed bishop on g7.

**18...♖ed8 19 ♗e4 ♖ac8 20 ♖ed1 ♘b6!**

From here the knight may go to a4 or c4. Preventing this with b2-b3 would only serve to weaken White's queenside structure – Black could contemplate hitting back with ...c6-c5.

**21 ♖e1 ♖d7 22 ♗f3 a5 23 ♖e2 a4**

For the last ten moves Black has been dictating the play completely, but White, despite all his meandering, still has a solid enough position. After White's next move, however, Black definitely has an advantage.

**24 a3?**

After this move the queenside is fixed and the black knight has permanent outposts on both c4 and d5. White was obviously afraid of Black playing ...a4-a3, but Finkel shows that White can survive after 24 ♖c1 a3 25 bxa3 (25 b3? c5 26 dxc5 ♖xc5 and the pressure on c3 will be unbearable) 25...♖a7 26 ♗d6 ♗f8 27 ♗b4 ♘c4. Black will recapture on a3 with a slight edge, but it's not too uncomfortable for White.

**24...♘c4 25 ♗f4 c5!**

Finally Black opens the position, but note that this is only executed after accomplishing some positional goals (clamping down on the queenside, outposts for the knight and a weak white pawn on b2 etc.).

**26 dxc5 ♖xc5 27 ♖c2 f5!**

Two further advantages for Black have been realised with the exchange of pawns: Black has control of the only open file, plus he can also begin to activate his newly formed pawn majority on the kingside. Suddenly it's Black who has all the space!

**28 ♗e2 e5 29 ♗xc4+**

White can stomach the knight no longer.

**29...bxc4 30 ♗e3 ♖cd5 31 f3 ♖d1+ 32 ♖xd1 ♖xd1+ 33 ♔f2 ♔f7 34 ♔e2 ♖d3 35 ♔f2 ♗f6**

Despite the simplification Black still holds all the positional trumps. White is severely cramped and his queenside majority is crippled by the black pawns on a4 and c4. White can do nothing but gradually watch Black improve his position.

**36 ♗c1 ♔e6 37 ♗e3 h5 38 ♔e2 ♗e7 39 ♔f2 ♔d5 40 ♔e2 e4**

**41 f4**

The exchange of rooks doesn't help White: 41 ♖d2 ♖xd2+ 42 ♔xd2 g5 (Black is virtually playing with an extra pawn) 43 ♔e2 (43 g4 hxg4 44 hxg4 exf3 45 gxf5 ♔e4 and Black wins – Finkel) 43...exf3+ 44 gxf3 g4 with a winning endgame, for example 45 hxg4 fxg4 46 fxg4 hxg4 47 ♗f4 ♔e4 48 ♗h2 ♗g5 49 ♗d6 ♗f4 50 ♗c5 g3 51 ♗b6 g2 52 ♗g1 ♗c1 53 ♗c5 ♗xb2 54 ♔f2 ♗xc3 55 ♔xg2 ♗d4 56 ♗b4 c3 57 ♔f1 c2 58 ♗d2 ♔d3 59 ♗c1 ♗e3.

**41...h4!**

Finkel gives an exclamation mark to this move, which cements White's g-pawn to g2 and leaves the f4-pawn vulnerable to a later attack.

**42 ♖d2 ♗d6 43 ♖d1**

43 ♖xd3+ is equivalent of resignation: 43...cxd3+ 44 ♔d2 ♗c5 45 ♗xc5 ♔xc5 and White is lost – 46 ♔e3 ♔c4 47 ♔d2 ♔b3 is zugzwang!

**43...♗c5**

It's true Black possesses the 'good' bishop and White has the 'bad' one, but here Black's easiest way through is to exchange them.

**44 ♗xc5**

Or 44 ♗c1 ♖xd1 45 ♔xd1 e3 46 ♔e2 ♔e4 and Black wins – Finkel.

**44...♔xc5 45 ♖d2**

If White avoids the exchange of rooks, Black has a safe way to win by simply utilising his pawn majority with ...g6-g5. White can only sit and watch this happen, for example 45 ♖b1 ♔d5 46 ♖e1 ♔e6 (46...e3?! 47 ♔f3! is not so clear) 47 ♖f1 ♔f6 48 ♖c1 g5 49 ♖f1

gxf4 50 ♖xf4 ♔g5 51 ♖f1 f4 52 ♖g1 ♔f5 53 ♖f1 e3 54 ♖d1 (54 ♔f3 ♖d2 is zugzwang) 54...♔e4.

**45...♔d5**

**46 ♖d1**

46 ♖xd3+ cxd3+ 47 ♔d2 ♔c5! 48 ♔e3 ♔c4 49 ♔d2 ♔b3 is again zugzwang.

**46...♖xd1 0-1**

After 47 ♔xd1 Black wins with 47...e3, followed by ...♔e4. Excellent position play by Tunik throughout the game, and a demonstration that the bishops don't always have it their own way, even when the position isn't particularly blocked.

# CHAPTER FOUR

## Strong Pawns and Weak Pawns

Philidor, probably the best chess player in the 18th century, once said that 'pawns are the soul of chess'. More than a century after Philidor's statement and well into the Romantic era, most of the world's top players were still treating pawns with disrespect, gambiting the foot soldiers as soon as possible in order to pursue attacks with pieces. Only later did the world elite come to the same conclusions as Philidor and finally players realised the correct way to treat pawns.

Pawn formations are just as important as piece formations The recognition of certain patterns of pawns and knowing how to treat them often separate the best from the merely very good. In this section we will be dealing with many of the different pawn formations that occur in chess practice.

### Pawn Islands

We often hear grandmasters referring to 'pawn islands', with sayings such as 'Black stands better as he has fewer pawn islands'. But what are they exactly?

The simplest way for me to explain is by an example.

Looking at the diagram position, we see there are many different types of pawn structures, all of which we will be examining in this section. White has three pawn islands: the a3-b2-c3 structure, the f2-f3 structure and the lone h2 pawn. Similarly, Black also has three pawn islands: the lone a4-pawn, the lone d5-pawn and the g7-g6-h7 structure. If you were to move the g6-pawn to f7 and the a4-pawn to e6, then Black would have just one pawn island and a very solid structure. So, in general, it's better to have fewer pawn islands.

The pawns on a4, d5 and h2 are isolated pawns; they have no neighbouring pawns of the same colour on adjacent files. This makes them weak as they cannot be protected by their own pawns. The pawn on d5 is particularly weak as it also stands on a half-open file. This means that White can attack it by the simple mechanism of putting a rook on the d-file.

Black's g-pawns are doubled. White's f-pawns are both doubled and isolated. As well as this, they also stand on a semi-open file. These three factors combine to make them extremely weak. Black's g-pawns are not so weak because the front pawn is defended by the h7-pawn. If the h7-pawn were to move to h5, then the g6-pawn would become very vulnerable, especially since it is situated on a half-open file.

Finally, the b2-pawn is known as a backward pawn. It has neighbours on adjacent files but these cannot protect it as they are too far forward. The weakness of this pawn is again increased owing to the fact that it's on a half-open file.

## Doubled Pawns

As we've seen before, doubled pawns are two pawns of the same colour on the same file. They can be weak in two different ways. The first of these is that they can be vulnerable to attack (see the previous diagram for such a case). The second weakness is that they can decrease the mobility of a pawn formation. The following example serves as an illustration of their weakness, even when they are not easy to attack.

The diagram shows a typical pawn structure arising from the Exchange Variation of the Ruy Lopez (1 e4 e5 2 ♘f3 ♘c6 3 ♗b5 a6 4 ♗xc6 dxc6 and White follows up with an early d2-d4). Black's doubled c-pawns are difficult to attack as the front pawn is defended by the b7-pawn, while they also do not stand on a half-open file.

The main weakness of the doubled c-pawn shows itself when Black tries to exploit his pawn majority on the queenside. Taking only pawn moves into consideration, if White were to adopt a formation of a3-b2-c3 (or a4-b3-c4) there would be no way for Black to force the creation of a passed pawn on the queenside. White, on the other hand, can easily create a passed pawn on the kingside. It's unsurprising, therefore, that virtually all king and pawn endings with this structure are winning for White. Of course, in the Exchange Variation of the Ruy Lopez White has a lot of work to do before he can reach something similar to the diagram; he also has to give up the bishop pair as early as the fourth move.

## Exploiting Weak Doubled Pawns

The diagram position tells a very sorry

story from White's point of view. He is at the moment a pawn to the good, but this is only temporary, as the e6-pawn will not last much longer.

**Shneider-Parker**
Port Erin 1999

The main problems for White, however, are his static weaknesses, including the miserable set of doubled and isolated c-pawns. Not only are they vulnerable to attack, they are completely immobile and they also leave gaps around the white king. Added to this, Black's knight has already found itself a great outpost on c5, where it is completely invulnerable to white pawns.

**20...♖de8**

Unsurprisingly, Black's first target is White's advanced e6-pawn.

**21 ♖he1 ♖hg8 22 ♗g1 ♔b8!**

In some lines Black can play ...♗c8 to increase the pressure on e6.

**23 ♖d2 ♘xe6!**

Tactics tends to work in good positions and this case is not an exception. Black picks up the e6-pawn without much effort, as after 24 ♘xe6 ♕xc3+ 25 ♖c2 ♕a3+ 26 ♔b1 ♖xg2! 27 ♕xg2 ♕b4+ Black picks up the rook on e1 and

the knight on e6.

**24 ♔b2 ♘g7 25 ♕d1**

**25...♕f7!**

This is the first real sign of pressure against the c4-pawn, which is the more vulnerable of White's two c-pawns.

**26 ♖xe8+ ♖xe8 27 ♕a4 ♘e6 28 ♘c6+ ♗xc6 29 ♕xc6 ♘d8 30 ♕d5 ♕g6!**

Naturally Parker refrains from capturing on d5, as this would help White to straighten his pawns out after cxd5.

**31 ♖c2 ♖e5 32 ♕d2 ♕f7**

There is no respite. Once again the c4-pawn is attacked.

**33 ♕d3 ♘c6**

The knight plans to go to a5, when the pawn will be lost. Notice how ineffective the white bishop is.

**34 ♖e2 ♕e6**

34...♘a5 is just as good.

**35 ♖xe5 ♘xe5**

The c4-pawn drops and the game is effectively over. Straightforward technique from Black has netted him a winning position.

**36 ♕e4 ♘xc4+ 37 ♔c1 ♘e5 38 ♔b1 ♕g8 39 ♕e2 ♕d5 40 ♗d4 ♘c4 41 ♕e8+ ♔b7 42 ♔c2 ♕g5 43 ♕e2 d5 44 ♔c1 c5!**

The bishop isn't allowed to settle anywhere.

**45 ♗g1 ♛e5 46 ♛xe5 ♘xe5 47 ♔d2 ♔c6 48 ♗f2 a5 49 ♗h4 b5 50 ♗f6 ♔d6 51 ♗g7 h5 52 ♗f8+ ♔c6 53 ♗h6 ♘g6 54 g3 fxg3 55 hxg3 h4 56 gxh4 ♘xh4 57 f4 ♘f5 58 ♗g5 b4 59 a4**

Otherwise Black continues with ...♔b5-a4.

**59...bxa3 60 ♔c2 d4 61 cxd4 cxd4 62 ♗f6 a4 63 ♗d8 ♔b5 64 ♗f6 ♔c4 65 ♗d8**

**65...d3+ 0-1**

**The Weakness of the Square**

In *Easy Guide to the Nimzo-Indian* (1 d4 ♘f6 2 c4 e6 3 ♘c3 ♗b4) I highlighted

the weakness of the c3-c4 doubled pawn complex which White takes on after an early exchange on c3. Being further forward, the c4-pawn is the most vulnerable and often comes under early attack. However, another point I mentioned was that even if White manages the liquidate the doubled pawns via exchanges, very often the c4-square remains a weakness and can be used as an outpost by Black. I gave the following classic example, which I can't resist repeating here.

**Mattison-Nimzowitsch**
Karlsbad 1929

**15...♘a5 16 ♛b5 ♛xb5 17 cxb5 ♘c4**

It's true that White has avoided the loss of a pawn and has undoubled his c-pawns, but straightening out doubled pawns doesn't always guarantee that the problem will go away. In this example Black is left with a superb outpost for his knight on c4.

**18 ♗c1**

The bishop is forced back to a miserable square.

**18...a6! 19 bxa6 ♖xa6 20 dxc5 bxc5 21 ♘g2 ♘d5**

White has big weaknesses on a2 and c3, while his bishop on c1 is a useless piece. It's little wonder that that the game only lasts a few more moves.

**22 ♖d3 ♖fa8 23 e4 ♘e5! 0-1**

Black wins after 24 ♖d1 ♘xc3 25 ♖f1 ♖xa2.

### Poluljahov-Lopushnoy
### Smolensk 2000

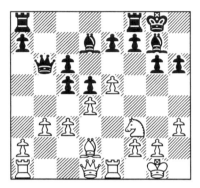

Here is another example of the same theme. Black is ready to exchange his forward doubled c-pawn for White's d-pawn. This can be seen as a small success for Black, but problems remain. The c-pawn disappears but the weakness of the c5-square does not go away.

**14 ♕c1!**

Hitting the h6-pawn and also preparing to put pressure on c5 with ♕a3.

**14...♔h7 15 ♕a3 cxd4 16 cxd4**

White has a clear advantage. Notice how the exchange of pawns has left White with a very useful half-open c-file, an outpost on c5 and a potentially vulnerable c6-pawn to attack.

**16...♖fe8**

The e7-pawn was attacked.

**17 ♖ac1 ♗f8 18 ♖c5!**

Using the outpost. This seems to set up a self-pin, but White has the situation firmly under control.

**18...♖eb8**

18...e6 wins the exchange, but capturing on c5 will leaves Black totally devastated on the dark squares, for example 19 ♕c1 ♗xc5? 20 dxc5 ♕b5 21 ♗xh6 and White will follow up with ♕g5-h4 and then ♗g5-f6. Black has no chance to survive this mating attack as he has absolutely no influence on the dark squares (a consequence of grabbing the rook on c5).

**19 ♕c1 ♗g7 20 ♕c2 ♗f5 21 ♕c3 ♖c8 22 ♘h4 ♗d7?**

This move allows a standard sacrificial breakthrough. The Israeli grandmaster Boris Avrukh suggests the more resilient 22...♗e6, although after 23 ♖c1 ♗d7 24 ♕d3, planning ♖1c3, ♕c2 and ♖g3, White keeps substantial advantage.

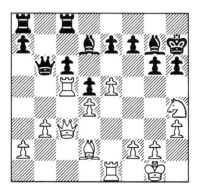

**23 e6!**

Inflicting Black with even more serious pawn weaknesses.

**23...♗xe6 24 ♖xe6! fxe6 25 ♕d3**

Black is the exchange up, but his pawn structure is a complete mess and, more importantly, nothing can be done to protect the crucial g6-pawn. With the removal of this pawn, Black's kingside is left defenceless.

**25...♕d8**

Or 25...♖f8 26 ♘xg6 ♖f6 27 ♘f8+ ♔g8 28 ♘d7 ♕b7 29 ♘xf6+ exf6 30 ♕g6 ♕f7 31 ♕g3 (Avrukh), with the twin threat of ♖xc6 and ♗xh6.

**26 ♕xg6+ ♔h8**

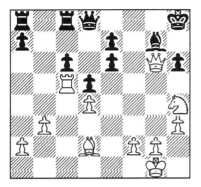

**27 ♖c3!?**

White's final piece joins into the attack on the kingside. 27 ♗xh6 is also very strong, for example 27...♕g8 28 ♕h5 ♗xh6 29 ♕xh6+ ♕h7 30 ♘g6+ ♔g8 31 ♘xe7+! ♕xe7 32 ♖c3 ♔f7 33 ♕h5+ ♔g8 34 ♖g3+ and White wins.

**27...♕e8**

Or 27...♕f8 28 ♖f3 ♗f6 29 ♗xh6 ♕g8 (29...♕e8 30 ♖xf6!) 30 ♕h5 and White wins (Avrukh).

**28 ♕xe6 ♗f6 29 ♖g3! 1-0**

Black has no good defence against the threat of 30 ♘g6+ ♔h7 31 ♕f5, followed by a devastating discovered check.

**Double Pawns as a Strength**

So far we've only looked at the negative side of passed pawns, but there are some positives too. Doubled pawns, especially ones on in the centre, can control vital squares. If you look back at the game Morozevich-Piket on page 56, you will see that Piket's doubled pawns actually strengthened his structure and added more control over central squares (this is why, in general, it is better to recapture towards the centre – Piket played ...bxc6, ...c6-c5 and ...axb6 to achieve his pawn diamond).

Another positive feature is that the creation of doubled pawns automatically produces an open file for the possessor of the doubled pawns. This can be good news for the activity of the rooks.

Naturally each position has to be considered on its own merits, before deciding whether the doubled pawns are a weakness, a strength, or just plain irrelevant.

**Emms-A.David**
Andorra 1998

In this position White's doubled c-pawns are by no means a weakness. The forward c-pawn is well protected by the pawn on b4 and has a good cramping effect on Black's position (Black cannot use the d6-square, for example). The c3-pawn completes the chain by defending b4 and cannot be easily attacked. As well as this, the c-pawns help to make a 4-2 pawn majority on the queenside for

White, and this is where he will turn his attention. It's true that Black has a 3-1 pawn majority on the kingside, including an outside passed pawn. However, with plenty of pieces remaining, White's advanced pawns are more dangerous.

**16 ♔c2 ♗e7 17 ♗g5 h6 18 ♗xe7 ♘xe7 19 ♘d4**

Using the protection of the c3-pawn to good effect by claiming an outpost in the centre of the board.

**19...♘d5 20 a3**

Preventing Black's threat of ...♘xb4+. 20 ♘xe6 fxe6 21 ♖xe6 wins a pawn, but after 21...♖hf8 Black has some annoying threats.

**20...♘f4 21 ♗e4 ♗d7 22 a4**

With the idea of ♘b5.

**22...a6**

Black sensibly avoids the threat. After 22...h5 23 ♘b5 ♗xb5 24 axb5 White opens up another avenue of attack and Black is hard pushed to defend, for instance 24...♔b8

25 ♗xb7! ♔xb7 26 ♖e7+ ♔b8 27 ♖axa7 gives White a winning attack – following 27...♘d5 28 ♖eb7+ ♔c8 29 c6 Black will soon be mated. This is certainly an occasion of the strength of the doubled pawns!

**23 ♘f5 ♗xf5 24 ♗xf5+ ♔b8 25 ♖e7**

Preparing ♗e4.

**25...♖hf8 26 c4**

The pawn mass continues to march forward.

**26...♖de8 27 ♖ae1 ♘e6 28 ♖xe8+ ♖xe8 29 ♔c3 g6 30 ♗h3 ♖d8?**

In time trouble my opponent tries a dubious pawn sacrifice. Black should begin counterplay on the queenside with 30...h5!.

**31 ♗xe6 ♖e8 32 ♖h1 ♖xe6 33 ♖xh6 ♖f6 34 b5**

Rather than defending passively with 34 ♖h2, White returns the pawn in order to reactivate the queenside majority.

**34...♔c7**

Or 34...♖xf2 35 ♖h8+ ♔c7 36 b6+ ♔d7 37 ♖b8 ♔c6 38 ♖c8+ ♔d7 39 ♖c7+ and the crucial b7-pawn drops.

**35 ♖h8 axb5 36 axb5**

On this occasion, keeping the doubled c-pawn is the easiest way to win!

**36...b6 37 c6! ♖f3+ 38 ♔b4 ♖xf2 39 ♖a8 g5 40 ♖a7+ ♔c8**

**41 c5! 1-0**

Fittingly, the doubled c-pawns have the final say. On first sight resignation seems a little premature, but there is no way out, for example 41...♖b2+ (or

41...bxc5+ 42 ♔xc5 ♖c2+ 43 ♔b6) 42 ♔c4 ♖c2+ 43 ♔d5 ♖xc5+ (43...bxc5 44 b6 wins) 44 ♔d6 ♔b8 45 ♖b7+ ♔c8 46 ♖xf7 ♔b8 47 ♖f8+ ♔a7 48 c7 and White wins.

In the following example White gladly accepts doubled pawns in order for more central control and a half-open file.

### Kindermann-Timman
Biel 1995
*Ruy Lopez*

**1 e4 e5 2 ♘f3 ♘c6 3 ♗b5 a6 4 ♗a4 ♘f6 5 0-0 b5 6 ♗b3 ♗c5 7 a4 ♗b7 8 d3 d6 9 ♘c3 b4 10 ♘d5 h6 11 a5 0-0 12 c3 ♖b8 13 ♗e3**

A typical move in this type of position. Kindermann gladly offers Black the chance to inflict doubled pawns on him.

**13...♘xd5 14 ♗xd5 ♗xe3 15 fxe3**

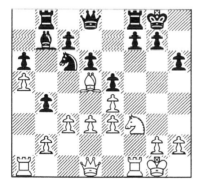

So White has doubled e-pawns, but they are hardly vulnerable to attack and they protect many important squares in the centre. As well as this, White can now utilise the half-open f-file, another consequence of capturing on e3.

**15...♘e7?!**

It has since been discovered that Black can equalise with the little trick: 15...bxc3

16 bxc3 ♘xa5! 17 ♖xa5 c6, with a double attack on a5 and d5.

**16 ♗c4!**

White's bishop, which pressurises both f7 and a6, is stronger than its black counterpart, hence White avoids the exchange.

**16...c5?!**

Now White can start a full scale assault on the f7-pawn. Kindermann offers 16...bxc3 17 bxc3 c6, preparing ...d6-d5, as an improvement.

**17 cxb4 cxb4 18 ♕b3! ♘c6**

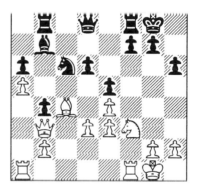

Menacing ...♘xa5, but White has his own threats...

**19 ♗xf7+!**

This idea works as a result of White possessing the half-open f-file.

**19...♖xf7 20 ♘g5 ♕xg5 21 ♕xf7+ ♔h8?**

Timman errs in a difficult position. Black can minimise White's advantage with 21...♔h7, for example 22 ♖f3 ♕e7 23 ♕f5+ ♔g8 24 ♖af1 ♖e8!? 25 ♕g6 (threatening ♖f7; Black's next move is forced) 25...♘d8 and White is better after either 26 ♖f6 ♗c6 27 ♖xd6 ♗b5 or 26 ♖g3 ♖f8 27 ♖xf8+ ♕xf8 28 ♕xh6, but Black is still alive and kicking.

**22 ♖f3 ♕d8?!**

Black's last chance was with 22...♕e7 23 ♕g6 ♕g5 (23...♖f8 24 ♖xf8+ ♕xf8 25 ♖f1 ♕g8 26 ♕xd6 wins) 24 ♕xd6 ♕d8!? 25 ♕d5 ♕e8, intending the trick 26 ♖af1? ♘d4! 27 ♖f8+ ♕xf8 28 ♖xf8+ ♖xf8 29 ♕xb7 ♘e2+ and mate next move. White, however, keeps a big advantage with 26 ♕c5!.

**23 ♖af1 ♗c8 24 ♕g6 1-0**

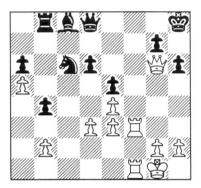

After 24...♗b7 25 ♖f7 ♕g8 26 ♖1f6! there is no good defence to the threat of ♕xh6+!.

### Isolated Pawns

A pawn is isolated if it has no neighbouring pawns of the same colour on adjacent files. This means it cannot be protected by pawns and can be vulnerable.

In the diagram position all six pawns are isolated. The pawns on d5,f5, e3 and g3 are especially vulnerable as they stand on half-open files. The two b-pawns are not so weak as they partially shield each other from attack.

On the positive side, by definition, the occurrence of an isolated pawn creates two adjacent open files for the possessor. The pawn also controls a square on each of these adjacent files (for example, the f5-pawn controls both e4 and g4). The further up the board the isolated pawn is, the stronger its influence – the d4-pawn controls both c3 and e3, points well within the enemy camp.

### Attacking Isolated Pawns

As I've said before, isolated pawns are much more easily attacked if they stand on a half open file as the attacker can simply move his rooks to this file and the pawn is under threat. Even when the pawn can be adequately defended, the fact that the possessor of the isolated pawn has to use pieces to defend it means that he will be passively placed for operations on other parts of the board.

In the following game Vladimir Kramnik slowly but surely exploits his opponent's isolated pawns to the full.

### Kramnik-Hjartarson
European Club Cup, Clichy 1995
*English Opening*

**1 ♘f3 c5 2 c4 ♘c6 3 ♘c3 ♘f6 4 g3 d5 5 d4!?**

Surprisingly this reaction in the centre was only introduced at the top level in 1988, when Tal tried it and won a nice game against Timman. Nowadays it's quite a fashionable line.

**5...cxd4**

Tal-Timman, Hilversum 1988 continued 5...dxc4 6 d5 ♘a5 (6...♘b4?! 7 e4 ♗g4 8 ♗xc4! ♗xf3 9 ♕xf3 ♘c2+ 10 ♔f1 ♘xa1 11 e5 gives White a strong attack) 7 e4 b5 8 ♘xb5 ♘xe4 9 ♘e5 ♗d7 10 ♘xd7 ♕xd7 11 ♕a4 ♖b8 12 ♘c7+ ♔d8 13 ♘e6+ fxe6 14 ♕xa5+ ♕c7 15 ♕xc7+ ♔xc7 16 ♗f4+ ♘d6 17 0-0-0 and White had a very good position.

**6 ♘xd4 dxc4 7 ♘xc6 ♕xd1+ 8 ♘xd1 bxc6 9 ♗g2 ♘d5 10 ♘e3 e6 11 ♘xc4 ♗a6 12 b3 ♗b4+ 13 ♗d2**

A good time to stop and assess the position. The queens and a pair of minor pieces have been exchanged and both sides have developed the rest of the minor pieces. Structurally White has a slight advantage – White possesses two pawn islands (one is the e2-f2-g3-h2 complex and the other is a2-b3) whereas Black has three (a7, c6 and e6-f7-g7-h7).

Black has two isolated pawns. The weakness on a7 is not serious at the moment, as it's difficult for White to attack the pawn. The c6-pawn, however, is Black's main worry and the reason for White's overall edge in the position. It stands on a half-open c-file, so White has a fairly straightforward plan of attacking it with his rooks.

**13...♔e7**

Black can, if he wishes, inflict an isolated pawn onto White with 13...♗xc4 14 bxc4 ♗xd2+ 15 ♔xd2 ♘e7 16 ♖ab1 0-0-0+ 17 ♔c3. Black has, in effect, traded disadvantages – White now has a bishop versus knight in a reasonably open position and with pawns on both sides of the board.

**14 ♖c1**

Strangely enough, according to *Mega Database 2001*, Kramnik has reached this position on two other occasions – once as White and once as Black. His game against Hjartarson is the only one that produced a decisive result.

**14...♖ac8**

It's clear that the c6-pawn will require some support, but experts are still undecided as to which rook should go to c8. 14...♖hc8, leaving the b-file for the a8-rook, was the move which appeared in Kramnik's two other games in this line.

**15 ♗xb4+ ♘xb4 16 a3 ♘d5 17 ♘a5 c5 18 0-0**

The situation has clarified and one can see that the weakness of the c5-pawn remains the most important aspect of the position. Notice that this is an occasion where the knight on the edge of the board is doing a good job; White's knight on a5 controls both the c4-square (dissuading Black from playing ...c5-c4) and protects the b3-pawn, which would otherwise be vulnerable to a counterattack along the b-file.

**18...♖hd8 19 ♖c2 ♖c7?!**

In his notes to the game, Kramnik said that he was more afraid of Black transforming the situation with a pawn sacrifice. After 19...c4! 20 ♘xc4 ♘b6 21 ♖fc1 ♘xc4 22 bxc4 ♖c5 Black is a pawn down, but it is now *White* who has the isolated pawn. With this being both vulnerable and well blocked, it's not clear whether White can make any progress with his extra pawn.

**20 ♖fc1 ♖dc8**

Hjartarson has his c-pawn well defended, but as a consequence his rooks are passively placed. Kramnik keeps an advantage and now begins to gain some space.

**21 e4 ♘f6 22 f4!**

Supporting the e4-e5 advance.

**22...♗d3 23 e5 ♘d5**

At first sight 23...♘e4 looks okay, but

after 24 ♖b2! Black's minor pieces are clumsily placed and White has a direct threat of ♖d1. Black can defend against this with 24...f5, but 25 exf6+ ♘xf6 leaves Black with a second weakness for White to attack – the isolated pawn on e6.

**24 ♖b2!**

A very fine move from Kramnik, keeping the tension and forcing Black to defend with the greatest of care. Kramnik notes that the immediate 24 ♖d2 nets a pawn, but Hjartarson was ready with the simplifying 24...c4! 25 bxc4 ♗xc4 26 ♖xc4 ♖xc4 27 ♘xc4 ♖xc4 28 ♗xd5 exd5 29 ♖xd5 ♖a4 30 ♖d3 f6 31 exf6+ ♔xf6 32 ♔f2; although White is a pawn up, Black's rook is active and he has very good chances to hold this ending.

**24...c4?**

A mistake in time trouble. Black seeks to force a line similar to the last note, but Kramnik has seen that this time it's more favourable for White. Black should probably sit tight with 24...♗b5, after which White improves his king position with 25 ♔f2.

**25 bxc4 ♗xc4 26 ♖xc4 ♖xc4 27 ♘xc4 ♖xc4 28 ♖b7+ ♔e8 29 ♗xd5! exd5 30 ♖xa7**

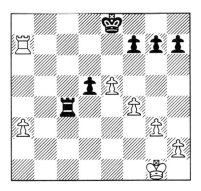

This rook ending is much more favourable for White, chiefly because Black's king is stuck on the back rank.

**30...d4 31 ♔f1 d3 32 ♔e1**

There is still time to ruin all the good work: 32 a4?? ♖e4 and the passed d-pawn cannot be stopped.

**32...♖c2 33 a4 ♖xh2 34 a5**

Material equality is re-established but White is winning – his outside passed a-pawn is much more threatening than Black's d-pawn.

**34...h5**

Or 34...g6 35 a6 ♖a2 36 ♖a8+ ♔e7 37 a7 h5 38 e6! (Kramnik) and White wins after:

a) 38...fxe6 39 ♖h8 ♖xa7 40 ♖h7+.

b) 38...♔xe6 39 ♖e8+.

c) 38...♖a3 39 exf7 ♔xf7 40 ♖h8 ♖xa7 41 ♖h7+.

**35 a6 ♖a2 36 f5! ♔f8**

Or 36...♖e2+ 37 ♔d1 ♖xe5 38 ♖b7 and a6-a7.

**37 ♔d1 g5 38 f6 ♔g8 39 ♖a8+ ♔h7 40 e6 1-0**

**The Isolated Pawn Couple**

The isolated pawn couple (or IPC as Alexander Baburin calls it) is a descendent of the isolated queen's pawn (or

IQP – see page 81) and arises if there is an exchange of pieces on c3 and a recapture with the b2-pawn (or ...bxc6 if Black has the isolated queen's pawn).

The first thing to notice is that White's pawn on d4 is now securely defended by the pawn on c3. However, the pawn on c3 is a backward pawn (see page 80) and is vulnerable in itself, especially since it stands on a half-open file.

The handler of the IPC has two main modes of playing this position. He can use the extra space to play for an attack on the kingside (as with the opening examples with the IQP). The other option is to play in the centre and advance the c-pawn to the fourth rank, thus creating the so-called 'hanging pawns' (see page 77).

Battling against the IPC (from Black's point of view), he must often defend against an assault on the kingside. As for the IPC itself, Black can attack it down the c-file and may also try to restrain it by controlling the key squares c4 and d5. Another idea is to smash the structure with either ...b6-b5-b4 or ...e6-e5.

In this first example we see White successfully going all out for a kingside attack.

**Poluljahov-Gomez Baillo**
Buenos Aires1998
*Caro-Kann Defence*

**1 c4 c6 2 e4 d5 3 exd5 cxd5 4 cxd5 ♘f6 5 ♘c3 ♘xd5 6 ♘f3 e6 7 ♗c4 ♗e7 8 0-0 0-0 9 d4 ♘xc3 10 bxc3 ♘c6 11 ♖e1 b6 12 ♗d3!**

White's light-squared bishop is well placed on d3, where it hits black's h7-pawn. White's strategy is quite straight-forward: he aims to attack Black on the kingside, where Black misses his normal defensive knight on f6.

**12...♗b7**

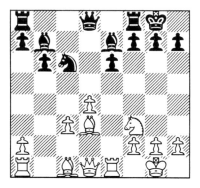

This theoretical position is a good iso-lated pawn couple position for White. The pawns in themselves are not particu-lar strong, but White's piece placement is superior to Black's. White has good prospects of a successful all-out mating attack on the kingside, which has much to do with Black lacking a defensive knight for cover. Transfer the black knight from c6 to f6 and Black would have far healthier prospects than he does in the diagram position.

**13 h4!**

Apparently it was the Russian grand-master Yuri Razuvaev who first intro-

duced this idea at the highest level. White prepares the aggressive move ♘g5, which will initiate dangerous threats against the black king. Of course Black can snatch the pawn on h4, but then White gains time and momentum for the attack by attacking the black queen.

**13...♗f6**

Black's alternatives are all risky:

a) 13...♗xh4 14 ♘xh4 ♕xh4 15 ♖e3 h6?! ( the lesser evil is 15...g6 16 ♖h3 ♕f6 17 ♗h6 ♖fe8 18 ♕g4 and White has a very dangerous attack, Kasparov-Gonda, Cannes {simul} 1988; the dark squares around Black's king are particu-larly vulnerable) 16 ♖h3 ♕f6 (16...♕e7 17 ♗xh6! gxh6 18 ♖xh6 is devastating, for example 18...♕g5 19 ♖h3 and Black has no good answer to ♖g3, pinning the queen) 17 ♕g4 g5 18 f4 and Black is in big trouble. The game Rabiega-R.Bauer, Germany 1996 concluded 18...♕g7 19 fxg5 f5 20 ♕e2 ♖ae8 21 ♖xh6 ♖f7 22 ♕h5 and Black resigned.

b) 13...♘a5! (I gave this as Black's best in *Attacking with 1 e4*) 14 ♘g5 and now:

b1) 14...h6 15 ♘h7! (suggested by Nunn; this is better than Razuvaev's 15 ♕h5, after which 15...♖ac8! is unclear) 15...♖e8 16 ♕g4 ♔h8

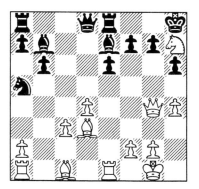

17 ♘g5! ♖f8 18 ♘xe6! fxe6 19 ♕g6 ♖f5 (or 19...♔g8 20 ♕h7+ ♔f7 21 ♗g6+ ♔f6 22 ♗h5) 20 ♖xe6 and White wins.

b) 14...g6 15 ♕g4! ♖c8 16 h5 ♖xc3 17 hxg6 ♖xd3 18 gxf7+ ♔h8 19 ♘xe6 with a winning position – Nunn.

c) 14...♗xg5 (this looks like Black's best bet) 15 ♗xg5 ♕d5 16 ♕g4 f5 17 ♕g3 with an edge to White, Poluljahov-Balashov, St. Petersburg 1998.

**14 ♘g5 g6**

14...h6 is asking for trouble, for example 15 ♕h5 (15 ♘h7 also looks good after 15...♖e8 16 ♕g4 ♔h8 17 ♘xf6 ♕xf6 18 ♕e4 ♕f5 19 ♕xf5 exf5 20 ♗f4) 15...♕d5? 16 ♗h7+ ♔h8 17 ♗e4 ♕a5 18 ♘xf7+ and White won quickly in Volodin-Grebionkin, Voronezh 2000.

**15 ♕g4 ♘e7?**

Black should play 15...h5!, although White still retains strong attacking chances with either 16 ♕g3 or 16 ♕h3.

**16 h5 ♘f5**

After something like 16...♕c7 17 hxg6 Black has no obvious way to recapture, as 17...hxg6 18 ♕h4! ♗xg5 19 ♗xg5, threatening ♗f6, is very strong for White.

**17 hxg6 hxg6**

**18 ♘xe6!**

It's not hard to believe that a sacrifice like this will work. Actually, 18 ♖xc6! fxe6 19 ♘xe6 (Nunn) is just as effective, for example 19...♕d5 20 ♕xg6+ ♘g7 (or 20...♗g7 21 ♗xf5 ♕xg2+ 22 ♕xg2 ♗xg2 23 ♘xf8) 21 ♘f4 ♕c6 22 ♗a3 (threatening 23 ♕h7+ ♔f7 24 ♗g6 mate) 22...♗e7 23 ♕h7+ ♔f7 24 ♗g6+ ♔f6 25 ♕h4 mate.

**18...fxe6 19 ♕xg6+ ♗g7**

Or 19...♘g7 20 ♗a3! (again with the idea of 21 ♕h7+ ♔f7 22 ♗g6 mate) 20...♗g5 21 ♖xe6 ♕d5 22 ♕h7+ ♔f7 23 ♖f6+! ♗xf6 24 ♗g6+ ♔e6 25 ♕h3+ ♘f5 26 ♗xf5+ ♕xf5 27 ♖e1+ and White wins.

**20 ♖xe6**

White now has three pawns for the piece, but more importantly, Black has no way of dealing with White's attack involving queen, rook and two bishops (with another rook handy if needed!).

**20...♕h4 21 ♗xf5 ♖xf5 22 ♕xf5 ♖f8 23 ♗g5 ♕h5 24 ♕g6 ♕xg6 25 ♖xg6 1-0**

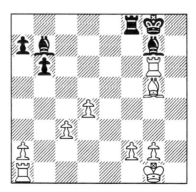

The following game from Karpov made a deep impression on me. It's a great demonstration of both light square domination and restraint of the isolated pawn couple.

**Taimanov-Karpov**
Moscow 1973
*Nimzo-Indian Defence*

1 d4 ♘f6 2 c4 e6 3 ♘c3 ♗b4 4 e3
c5 5 ♗d3 0-0 6 ♘f3 d5 7 0-0 dxc4
8 ♗xc4 cxd4 9 exd4 b6 10 ♕e2
♗b7 11 ♖d1 ♘bd7 12 ♗d2

This is a passive move, although I'm
loath to criticise it too much as it has
been used by many strong grandmasters.
If White is looking for a bit more action
he should consider the alternative 12
♘e5!.

**12...♖c8 13 ♗a6!?**

The point of White's previous move is
revealed – the light-squared bishop is
free to move. To merrily exchange pieces
in an IQP position goes against general
principles – the weakness of the isolated
pawn increases as the position simplifies.
On this occasion, however, White hopes
to cause some hassle on the queenside
with his queen.

**13...♗xa6 14 ♕xa6 ♗xc3**

Both 14...♖c7? and 14...♕c7 are met
by 15 ♘b5!, so this move is more or less
forced.

**15 bxc3**

Accepting the isolated pawn couple.
15 ♗xc3?! doesn't inspire much confi-
dence – the bishop looks like a big pawn
on c3. After 15...♕c7 16 ♖ac1 ♘d5 17
♗d2 ♕b8 Black has no problems,
Geller-Furman, Kiev 1957.

**15...♖c7**

A couple of exchanges has left us with
a deceptively simple position, in which
Karpov excels. For the moment it seems
that White has some annoying pressure
against the a7-pawn, but Karpov has a
very radical solution in mind.

**16 ♖ac1**

Preparing to advance with c3-c4 –
White wants to gain control over the
crucial central squares c4 and d5. 16 c4?
♕c8! would give White headaches over
his c4-pawn.

**16...♕c8 17 ♕a4**

Once again White prepares c3-c4. 17
♕xc8?! ♖fxc8 leaves Black in control, as
c3-c4 is prevented.

**17...♖c4!!**

This is Karpov's idea. The a7-pawn is
sacrificed, but in return Black obtains
total light-square domination and a iron-
like grip on White's isolated pawn couple.

**18 ♕xa7 ♕c6 19 ♕a3 ♖c8**

It's plain to see that White is already

condemned to a passive defence. Objectively speaking the position may well be equal, but I know which side most grandmasters would prefer to play.

**20 h3 h6 21 ⌐b1 ⌐a4 22 ⚌b3 ♘d5 23 ⌐dc1 ⌐c4 24 ⌐b2 f6**

Typical Karpov. Black could already recapture with 24...♘xc3 but Karpov prefers the bide his time. The pawn, after all, is going nowhere. Instead Karpov brings his king into the game, a sure sign of Black's dominance.

**25 ⌐e1 ♔f7 26 ⚌d1 ♘f8 27 ⌐b3 ♘g6!**

Continuing to tease White. This knight may want to jump into the f4-square.

**28 ⚌b1 ⌐a8 29 ⌐e4 ⌐ca4 30 ⌐b2 ♘f8 31 ⚌d3**

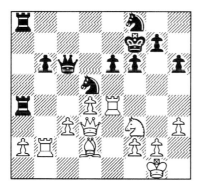

**31...⌐c4!**

A crucial point. Black could regain the pawn with 31...⌐xa2? but after 32 ⌐xa2 ⌐xa2 33 c4 Black's bind on the light squares is suddenly broken and he is forced to retreat.

**32 ⌐e1 ⌐a3 33 ⚌b1 ♘g6 34 ⌐c1 ♘xc3**

Finally Karpov cashes in to regain the pawn, while still retaining the pressure.

**35 ⚌d3**

35 ♗xc3 ⌐axc3 36 ⌐xc3? ⌐xc3 and suddenly White is facing a disastrous check on the back rank.

**35...♘e2+! 36 ⚌xe2 ⌐xc1+ 37 ♗xc1 ⚌xc1+ 38 ♔h2**

**38...⌐xf3!**

A shocking move, which was particularly effective due to White's major time trouble. White must capture with the pawn.

**39 gxf3 ♘h4**

and in this extremely difficult position Taimanov overstepped the time limit. Black is probably winning in any case, for example 39...♘h4 40 ⌐b3 or (40 ⌐xb6 ⚌c7+) 40...⚌g5 41 ⚌f1 ⚌f4+ 42 ♔h1 ♘xf3 43 ♔g2 ♘d2! An almost effortless performance from Karpov.

**Hanging Pawns**

This is a pawn island consisting of a pair of united pawns on half-open files. They often arise from isolated pawn couples.

*see following diagram*

The diagram shows White possessing the hanging pawns. Let's look at the positive features first. The pawns grant White a healthy space advantage and control many useful squares in the centre of the board. This may certainly help to restrict an opponent's mobility. On occasions one of the pawns may advance to support an attack and the d-pawn in particular can sometimes advance to cramp Black further or to create a passed pawn.

On the minus side, the pawns are again vulnerable to attack as they cannot be supported by neighbouring white pawns and they are also on half-open files. Black has a straightforward plan to pressurise them by putting his rooks on the c- and d-files. Black can also try to attack the pawns with either ...b5 or ...e5. However White reacts to these breaks, he will be left with some sort of weakness. An advance of either the d- or the c-pawn leaves the other one backward and also gives an outpost to the opposition. For example, if White plays d4-d5 then the c4-pawn is backward and the c5-square becomes an outpost for Black.

Here are two examples of games involving hanging pawns. In the first game Nigel Short perfectly demonstrates the attacking potential of the pair, while the second example shows a worst case scenario for the possessor – a simplified position where the weakness of the pawns becomes more important.

**Andersson-Short**
Thessaloniki Olympiad 1988
*Queen's Gambit Declined*

1 ♘f3 d5 2 d4 ♘f6 3 c4 e6 4 ♘c3 ♗e7 5 ♗g5 h6 6 ♗h4 0-0 7 e3 b6 8 ♖c1 ♗b7 9 a3 ♘bd7 10 cxd5 exd5 11 ♗e2 c5 12 0-0 ♘e4 13 ♗xe7 ♕xe7 14 dxc5 ♘xc3 15 ♖xc3 bxc5

White's play in the opening has been rather unambitious and Short has secured a comfortable game without too much difficulty. Black's pieces are well placed, the bishop protecting the d5-pawn and the knight protecting c5. Meanwhile, White will find it difficult to add any further pressure and will always have to be aware of Black advancing with ...d5-d4.
**16 ♕c2**
16 ♕a4, with ideas of ♕a5, looks more active.
**16...♖ab8!**
A commendable place for this rook. The bishop can drop back to a8, after which the rook will pressurise the slightly vulnerable b2-pawn.
**17 ♖c1**
17 ♗b5?, preparing to swap off the c5-protector, allows tactics after 17...d4!

18 exd4 ♗xf3 19 ♗xd7 ♗e4! and in all cases Black keeps the advantage:

a) 20 ♕a4 ♖fd8.

b) 20 ♖e1 ♗xc2 21 ♖xe7 ♖xb2.

c) 20 ♖e3 ♗xc2 21 ♖xe7 cxd4 – Flear.

**17...♗a8**

Now ♗b5 is prevented.

**18 b3 ♖fe8**

With the obvious idea of ...d5-d4.

**19 ♗f1 ♕d6 20 ♕d1 ♖ed8 21 ♘d2**

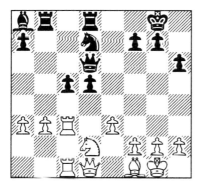

**21...d4!**

Black is now very well placed for this thematic advance.

**22 ♘c4 ♕f6 23 ♖d3 ♘f8!**

The knight is coming to e6 to further support d4.

**24 b4?**

This loses a pawn. The alternative 24 exd4 cxd4 gives Black a strong passed d-pawn, but this is probably White's best.

**24...dxe3 25 ♘xe3 cxb4 26 axb4 ♖xd3 27 ♕xd3 ♖xb4 28 ♖c8 ♗b7 29 ♘d5 ♗xd5 30 ♕xd5 ♕e7! 31 g3 g6 32 ♕c6 ♖d4 33 ♕c3 ♖d1 34 ♕c4 a5 35 ♖a8 ♕b4! 36 ♕a6 ♔g7 37 ♕e2 ♖c1 0-1**

White has no decent defence to Black gradually pushing the a-pawn through. A very smooth performance from Nigel Short

**Wojtkiewicz-Benjamin**
Pleasantville 1993

In this simplified position the hanging pawns are a real liability. The exchange of two pairs of knights has left Black without any space problems and both his bishops are superior to their opposite numbers. Black is free to concentrate his efforts on attacking the pawns on c4 and d4.

**24 ♗b2 ♖fe8**

24...♕c6?! allows the typical lunge with 25 d5!, for example 25...exd5 26 cxd5 ♕d6 27 ♗xg7 ♔xg7 28 ♗g2 and now White's passed pawn on d5 gives him the edge.

**25 ♗g2?!**

At first sight it seems only natural for White to fight for control of the long diagonal, but Benjamin actually criticises this move. The point is with the exchange of light-squared bishops, White will find it harder to defend his weak pawn on c4.

**25...♗xg2 26 ♔xg2 ♕b7+ 27 f3?**

This leaves White with a vulnerable king. 27 ♕f3 had to be tried, when Black can choose between 27...♕a6 and 27...♖e7 28 ♕xb7 ♖xb7 29 ♗a3 ♖d7.

**27...♕a6 28 ♖d3 ♖c7**

Preparing ...♖ec8. Black's position virtually plays itself, but he still has to be wary of cheap tactics, for example 28...♖xc4?? 29 ♖a3 and Black can resign. **29 ♖a3 ♕b7 30 ♖b3 ♖d8 31 ♖d3 ♕a6**

**32 ♔h3?**

Perhaps White was in time-trouble here, as this move looks very strange and it loses a pawn immediately. White should play another waiting move, although that's easier said than done. 32 ♖a3 ♕c8! is strong while 32 ♔g1 allows 32...♖xc4 – 33 ♖a3 ♖xc1+ is check.

**32...♕c8!**

With the double threat of ...e5+ and ...♖xc4. Black wins a crucial pawn.

**33 ♖dd1 e5+ 34 ♔g2 exd4 35 ♕d3 ♖e7 36 ♖e1 ♖e3! 37 ♕d2 h5 38 ♖cd1 ♖xe1 39 ♖xe1 ♕xc4 40 ♖e7 ♕xa2 0-1**

## Backward Pawns

A backward pawn is another type of pawn which cannot be defended by fellow pawns. The backward pawn has at least one neighbouring pawn of the same colour on an adjacent file, but this pawn(s) is too far forward to help in the backward pawn's defence. Also the backward pawn is restrained by an enemy pawn so that it cannot easily move forward to improve its position. Once again I find it easier by looking at a diagram.

In the diagram position there are four backward pawns, on c6, f6, e3 and g4. Each pawn is either blocked or restrained by an enemy pawn. The pawns on c6 and e3 are weaker than the other two as they also stand on half-open files and are thus vulnerable to attack by enemy rooks. If there were an exchange of pieces on the c5-square and White recaptured with the d-pawn, then the weakness of the c6-pawn would be masked by White's own pawn on c5.

There have already been many demonstrations of backward pawns in this book. I refer the reader to the section on outposts, with the many examples from the Sicilian Defence and the backward pawn on d6. In the case of Sicilian lines with ...e7-e5 for Black, the extra central pawn on d6 is well protected. As we saw earlier, often the key battle is for the square in front of the pawn.

An example of the backward pawn as a real weakness can be seen in the game Shirov-Short (see page 25).

# CHAPTER FIVE

## The Isolated Queen's Pawn

I've decided to devote a longer than normal part of the book to isolated queen's pawn (IQP) positions. They've always been of special interest to me and they occur so frequently in practice that they are worthy of a deep study. In fact, I know of at least one occasion where a whole book has been devoted to the IQP and its descendants. The book in question (*Winning Pawn Structures* by Alexander Baburin) can be heartily recommended to players with a keen interest in this subject. With just a small percentage of pages devoted to the IQP, I cannot hope to do such a totally comprehensive job, but I hope that I can point out most of the important features of this pawn structure.

To give you some idea of the popularity of IQP positions I should list some openings which can easily lead to IQPs: the English Opening, the Scandinavian Defence, the Caro-Kann, the c3-Sicilian, the French, the Petroff, the Queen's Indian and the Nimzo-Indian. And this is before I mention the many possible variations of the Queen's Gambit (Accepted or Declined)!

The diagram shows the most popular pawn structure of an IQP position (another less frequent version occurs where there is a c-pawn rather than an e-pawn, while yet another version has a black pawn on e7 and a fianchetto with ...g7-g6). Of course, there are also many occasion when it's Black who is the proud owner of the IQP.

Looking at the negative features first, it is quite clear that the d4-pawn can be vulnerable to attack. Of course it cannot be supported by pawns and it stands on a half-open file. If Black can line up his rooks on the d-file then White may be forced to passively defend his pawn. Another negative feature (from White's point of view) is that Black has control over the crucial d5-square, which can be used as a very effective outpost for a black piece, especially a knight.

On the positive side, the pawn on d4 controls two important squares. The e5-square is especially important and can become a useful outpost for a white knight. Another point is that the d4-pawn grants White a certain space advantage and good piece activity which can be important, especially when there are lots of pieces on the board. One final point (which is not obvious from just looking a the diagram) is that the IQP often arises with a development advantage for the possessor (the Queen's Gambit Accepted is one obvious example). In these cases the player with the IQP has an early initiative and possibly good attacking chances against the opposing king.

## Some Statistics

As with the bishop pair, I was very keen to carry out a statistical survey of results involving IQP positions. Once again using *Mega Database 2001* and some functions of *ChessBase*, I managed to come up with some answers, some of which are shown below.

| | Pawn structure | (a) moves 1-15 | (b) moves 16-25 | (c) moves 26-35 |
|---|---|---|---|---|
| 1 | W: d4 B: e6 | 53% (2346/2348) | 49% (2335/2342) | 46% (2327/2345) |
| 2 | W: d4 B: g6 & e7/e6 | 49% (2332/2336) | 49% (2339/2344) | 46% (2331/2346) |
| 3 | W: d5 B: e7 & g6 | 57% (2361/2351) | 56% (2361/2356) | 52% (2346/2350) |
| 4 | W: e3 B: d5 | 56% (2378/2361) | 59% (2374/2357) | 61% (2371/2351) |
| 5 | W: g3 & e2/e3 B: d5 | 61% (2383/2349) | 63% (2387/2361) | 63% (2384/2361) |
| 6 | W: g3, e2 B: d4 | 57% (2386/2358) | 57% (2389/2366) | 58% (2384/2362) |

The percentage score always refers to White's score

Numbers in brackets are average ratings of the players (White/Black)

There was a proviso that the structure existed for at least four half-moves.

First of all I will attempt to explain the table above. I took six test pawn structures (all IQPs) and examined them one by one. Taking, as an example, Test 1, I searched for all games with the IQP structure of a white pawn on d4 and a black pawn on e6 (as in the diagram on the previous page). In Test 2 I examined the case where Black had fianchettoed with ...g7-g6 and in Test 3 I examined the case with both a fianchetto and with White's pawn on d5. Tests 4-6 were the mirror image of the first three, with this time Black possessing the IQP.

However, I also tested for the creation and liquidation of the IQP. For example, in Test (a) the condition that had to be met was that the IQP was created in the first fifteen moves. In Test (c) the condition was that the IQP still existed after move 26.

## Results

Looking first at Test 1, White (the possessor of the IQP) scores just under average (53% as opposed to the average of 54%) when the IQP is created in the opening moves, but the score goes down if the IQP is still around from moves 16-25, and it goes down further if the IQP still exists later on in the game.

The same pattern is followed in Test 2, expect that White only scores 49% when the pawn is created within moves 1-15. Test 3 again follows a similar pattern to the first two test. The big difference here is that White's general score goes up considerably with the pawns on d5 and e7. In all the first three tests, the difference in the players' ratings is too insignificant to have any bearing on the results.

Tests 4-6 all show White scoring higher than average when he is facing the IQP. And once again the score against the IQP increases the longer in the game the IQP exists.

It's noticeable that in some cases in tests 4-6 the average rating of the white players is considerably higher than that of the black players. In these cases there

is a certain bearing on the results. For example the rating differences in tests 4(a), 5(a) and 6(a) imply that, with equally matched players, White's score would be much nearer to the average of 54%.

## Conclusions

Looking at test one, we can conclude that White's score is near enough average if the isolated pawn is created in the first fifteen moves. However, and this applies to all the tests, the score of the player in possession of the IQP goes down the longer the pawn remains on the board. If the IQP is either created or still exists between moves 26-35 then the overall result of the possessor is well below average. This result concurs with the theory that the weakness of the isolated pawn becomes more prominent as the game goes on and more pieces are exchanged. Also, a creation of an IQP later on in the game is less likely to be successful.

Another conclusion that we can make is that the score of the player fighting against the IQP increases if he fianchettoes with g2-g3 (or ...g7-g6 as Black). This is a logical result because the fianchettoed bishop has good defensive qualities and directly attacks the weakness of the IQP (see Karpov-Kasparov on page 105). However, with the fianchetto, the results of the possessor of the IQP increase when the pawn exists on d5 with White (and d4 with Black). Again this seems to make some sense as these situations give the players with the IQP even more space.

## Attacking with the IQP

That's enough facts and figures. Let's now look at a few examples from practical play. Firstly, I would like to concentrate on examples where the possessor of the IQP is attacking. These cases usually occur when the possessor of the IQP has a development advantage and can utilise this to achieve an early initiative.

**Stoica-Flis**
Polanica Zdroj 1983
*Caro-Kann Defence*

1 e4 c6 2 d4 d5 3 exd5 cxd5 4 c4 e6 5 ♘c3 ♘f6 6 ♘f3 ♗e7 7 cxd5 ♘xd5 8 ♗d3 0-0 9 0-0 ♘c6 10 ♖e1 ♘f6 11 a3

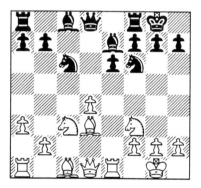

A typical IQP starting position, which most theoretical works judge to be in White's favour (White scores 59% in *Mega Database 2001*). White's last move paves the way for ♗c2 and ♕d3, lining up a dangerous attack on the h7-pawn.
**11...b6 12 ♗c2**

A refinement is 12 ♗g5 ♗b7 and only then 13 ♗c2 – see the next note.
**12...♗b7**

Theory now considers 12...♗a6! to be more accurate, as this cuts across White's basic plan of ♕d3.
**13 ♕d3**

This is now a very promising position for White. In *Mega Database 2001* White has scored an impressive 70% from here. However, it must be admitted that part of the reason for such good white results is that this move conceals a well-hidden idea.
**13...♖e8?**

This innocent-looking move is virtually a decisive mistake. Other moves include:

a) 13...♖c8? is natural but meets the same fate: 14 d5! exd5 (14...♘b8 is relatively best, after which 15 dxe6 ♕xd3 16 ♗xd3 ♗xf3 17 exf7+ ♖xf7 18 gxf3 gives White 'only' has a clear advantage) 15 ♗g5 ♘e4 (15...g6 16 ♖xe7! ♕xe7 17 ♘xd5 is one of White's ideas) 16 ♘xe4 dxe4 17 ♕xe4 g6 18 ♗h6 ♖e8 19 ♖ad1 ♕c7 20 ♗b3! (with a big threat of ♗xf7+) 20...♘d8 21 ♕d4 and Black was forced to resign in W.Schmidt-Imanaliev, Moscow Olympiad 1994.

b) 13...g6 is Black's best move, after which White has to make do with a moderate advantage, for example 14 ♗h6 ♖e8 15 ♖ad1 ♖c8 16 ♗b3 (now the b1-h7 diagonal has been blocked, the bishop changes direction – this is quite a common idea) 16...♘a5 17 ♗a2 ♘d5 18 ♘e5 ♗f8 (18...♘xc3? 19 ♘xf7!) 19

♗xf8 ♖xf8 20 ♘e4 was a bit better for White in the game Luther-Gheorghiu, Lenk 1999 – Black has succeeded in exchanging a pair of minor pieces, but the dark-squared weaknesses around his king are a cause for concern.

**14 d5!**

The classic d4-d5 breakthrough, a massive attacking tool of the player with the IQP. On this occasion it is devastatingly strong and emphasises the potential in White's position.

**14...♙xd5**

It's difficult to believe, but Black is virtually lost after this move. Alternatively 14...♘a5 15 b4 wins material for White. Relatively best is 14...♘b8 15 dxe6 fxe6 16 ♘d4, when White has a very strong position.

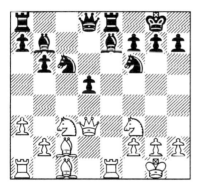

**15 ♗g5**

Simply threatening ♗xf6, followed by ♕xh7+.

**15...♘e4**

Or 15...g6 16 ♖xe7! ♘xe7 (16...♕xe7 17 ♘xd5 ♘xd5 18 ♗xe7 ♘cxe7 gives Black insufficient material for the queen; White must be winning in the long run) 17 ♗xf6 ♕d6 18 ♗e5 ♕e6 19 ♘b5 ♗a6 20 ♕d2 and Black resigned in Ong-Olsen, Espoo 2000 on account of 20

♕d2 ♗xb5 21 ♕h6 f6 22 ♘g5!.

**16 ♘xe4 dxe4 17 ♕xe4 g6 18 ♕h4**

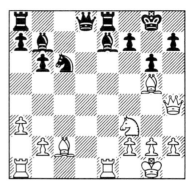

The centre has been cleared and White is left with a winning initiative – both ♖ad1 and ♗b3 are coming.

**18...♕c7**

18...♗xg5 19 ♘xg5 h5 20 ♗xg6! is very strong. After 20...fxg6 21 ♕c4+ ♔g7 22 ♕f7+ ♔h6 23 ♕xb7 ♕xg5 24 ♕xc6 White is a clear pawn up and Black's king is still vulnerable, Demarre-Chaumont, Paris 1991.

**19 ♗b3!**

Threatening ♗xf7+

**19...h5**

19...♗d6 20 ♗f6 (with the idea of ♘g5) 20...h5 21 ♕g5 ♔h7 22 ♗c2 was the end of Dizdar-Dizdarevic, Sarajevo 1988 – ♕xh5+ is coming.

**20 ♕e4**

Another threat – this time it is ♕xg6+.

**20...♔g7 21 ♗xf7!**

All the tactics work for White.

**21...♔xf7 22 ♗h6!**

Threatening ♕e6 mate and ♕c4+.

**22...♕d7 23 ♕c4+ ♔f6 24 ♕c3+ ♘d4**

It's mate after 24...♔f7 25 ♕g7.

**25 ♘xd4 ♔f7 26 ♘f3 ♗f8 27 ♗xf8 1-0**

White checkmates after 27...♚xf8 28 ♕h8+ ♚f7 29 ♘g5. This game serves as a chilling reminder of White's potential attacking chances in certain IQP positions.

**Emms-Sagall**
London (rapidplay) 1995
*Sicilian Defence*

**1 e4 c5 2 c3 ♘f6 3 e5 ♘d5 4 ♘f3 ♘c6 5 ♗c4 ♘b6 6 ♗b3 d5 7 exd6 e6**

Both 7...♕xd6 and 7...c4 are probably stronger. After the text move we soon reach an IQP position in which Black's g8-knight has moved three times to reach b6, whereas it would prefer now to be back on f6!

**8 d4 cxd4 9 cxd4 ♗xd6 10 0-0 0-0 11 ♖e1 ♘d5 12 ♘c3 ♘ce7**

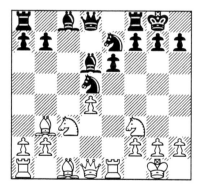

We are only just out of the opening phase, but we can already say that this is a very pleasant IQP position for White. Firstly, no minor pieces have been exchanged and White's are all actively placed. Another point in White's favour is that Black has adopted an essentially passive stance. True, Black has blockaded the d-pawn, but by simply blockad-ing Black has no immediate pressure on the pawn. Because of this, White doesn't have to worry about protecting d4 so his pieces have a free reign. One final problem for Black, which was mentioned before, is that he is missing the useful defending knight on f6.

**13 ♗g5**

A natural and aggressive move. By pinning the e7-knight to the queen, White adds extra pressure to the crucial d5-square.

**13...♕b6 14 ♕d3**

An active place for the queen, eyeing the h7-square and introducing ideas such as ♗c2.

**14...♗d7 15 ♖ad1**

On first sight 15 ♖ac1, moving the rook to the open c-file, seems more natural. This, however, would only encourage eventual exchanges on the c-file (Black would hurry to contest the file with ...♖ac8). Indeed, in many IQP positions the a1-rook belongs on d1. Obviously protecting the d4-pawn is useful, but the main point is that an eventual d4-d5 will carry more weight with a rook behind the pawn.

**15...♗c6**
Bolstering the d5-square.

15...罝ac8 allows White to show a point of his previous move: 16 奧xe7! ②xe7 17 d5 exd5 18 ②xd5 ②xd5 19 豐xd5 罝c6 20 ②g5 and the opening up of the position has greatly favoured White.

15...②xc3 16 bxc3 is playable for Black, but note that 16...奧c6? is answered by 17 d5!, when 17...②xd5 18 c4 wins material, as does 17...奧xd5 18 奧xe7 奧xb3 19 ②g5!.

**16 奧xe7! ②xe7**

Of course 16...奧xe7 17 ②xd5 loses a piece.

**17 ②g5!**

Punishing Black for the lack of a defensive knight on f6.

**17...②g6**

Or 17...g6 18 ②xe6! fxe6 19 罝xe6 and White threatens both 20 罝xd6+ and 20 罝xe7+.

**18 罝xe6!**

On this occasion White can sacrifice a rook to break up Black's kingside pawn structure.

**18...fxe6 19 豐h3**

The correct way to continue the attack. Black survives after 19 奧xe6+? 含h8 20 豐xg6? hxg6 21 罝d3 奧f3!.

**19...罝f6!**

The best defensive try. 19...h6 20 豐xe6+ 含h8 21 豐xg6 is very nasty for Black, as 21...hxg5 allows mate with 22 豐h5.

**20 奧xe6+ 含f8**

20...罝xe6 allows White a typical smothered mate with 21 豐xe6+ 含h8 22 ②f7+ 含g8 23 ②h6+ 含h8 24 豐g8+! 罝xg8 25 ②f7.

**21 ②xh7+ 含e7 22 ②xf6 gxf6 23 豐h7+ 含xe6 24 d5+ 奧xd5 25 ②xd5**

**25...豐xb2?**

The last chance for Black was with 25...罝h8!, after which White must choose between a very favourable ending after 26 豐xh8 ②xh8 27 ②xb6 axb6, or 26 豐xg6 奧xh2+ 27 含f1 豐b5+ 28 罝d3, when White's attack should prevail.

**26 豐xg6**

This is good enough, although my *Fritz* computer engine typically spots a quick checkmate in four with 26 ②c7+! 奧xc7 27 豐d7+ 含e5 28 罝d5+ 含f4 29 豐f5.

**26...罝h8 27 豐g4+ 含e5 28 ②e3 1-0**

In the following game White uses the well-known technique of swinging the rook over to the kingside in order to join the attack.

**Yevseev-Kyprijanov**
St Petersburg 2000
*Queen's Gambit Accepted*

**1 d4 d5 2 c4 dxc4 3 e3 ♘f6 4 ♗xc4 e6 5 ♘f3 c5 6 0-0 a6 7 ♗b3**

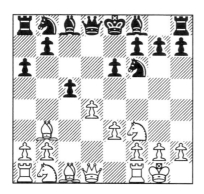

A prophylactic action. White takes measures against Black's plan of ...b7-b5. This is currently a fashionable line of the Queen's Gambit Accepted.

**7...♘c6**

7...b5 8 a4! is known to be good for White.

**8 ♕e2**

Deciding to put the rook on d1 to support the d4-pawn and the d4-d5 thrust. 8 ♘c3 cxd4 9 exd4 ♗e7 10 ♖e1 0-0 leads to a similar position.

**8...cxd4 9 ♖d1 ♗e7**

If Black wishes to avoid the upcoming IQP position then he can play 9...d3!? 10 ♖xd3 ♕c7.

**10 exd4 0-0**

A natural move, but possibly a mistake! Current theory approves of immediate queenside action with 10...♘a5 (threatening to exchange White's important light-squared bishop) 11 ♗c2 b5 12 ♘c3 ♗b7 and Black has the d5-square under reasonable control, Illescas Cor-

doba-Anand, Leon (2nd matchgame) 1997. If White now plays 13 ♘e4 then 13...♘xe4 14 ♗xe4 0-0 is okay for Black (compare with the note to Black's 11th move).

**11 ♘c3**

Now Black must already be aware of a possible d4-d5 break by White.

**11...♘b4**

11...b5? invites trouble after 12 d5! exd5 13 ♘xd5 – Black's lack of development causes him many headaches, for example 13...♘xd5? 14 ♗xd5 and White wins a piece.

11...♘a5 12 ♗c2 b5 takes the sting out of a d4-d5 break, but 13 ♘e4!? seems to favour White, who can use the c5-square as an outpost: 13...♗b7 (of course not 13...♘xe4?? 14 ♕xe4 and White wins) 14 ♘c5 ♗d5 15 ♘e5 and White has an edge, I.Sokolov-Volzhin, Koge 1997. Nevertheless, I prefer 11...♘a5 to the text.

**12 ♘e5 ♘bd5**

Another favourable IQP position for White. Black has managed to blockade the d-pawn, but at a cost of development elsewhere (Black's light-squared bishop and a8-rook are still at home). As well as this, Black has no actual pressure on the pawn itself (at this moment no piece attacks it). This gives White a free reign to attack.

### 13 ♖d3!

Transferring the rook to the third rank and preparing to swing it over to the kingside. This 'rook lift' can be a potent weapon for the possessor of the IQP. On this occasion White's attack against the black king will certainly gain lots of momentum with ♖f3, ♖g3 or ♖h3. Note, however, that it is only Black's lack of pressure against the d4-pawn which allows White to proceed with such an extravagant attacking idea.

### 13...♕d6

Alternatively:

a) 13...♗d7 14 ♖g3 (with ideas of ♗h6) 14...g6 (14...♖c8? 15 ♗h6 ♘e8 16 ♗xg7 ♘xg7 17 ♕g4 ♗f6 18 ♘xd5 is winning for White) 15 ♗h6 ♖e8 16 h4! (the caveman approach – White uses his h-pawn as a 'battering ram' to soften up Black's kingside) 16...♗f8 17 ♗g5 ♕c7? (17...♗c6 is more resilient) 18 ♕f3 ♗g7 19 ♗xd5 and Black resigned in Filip-Conrady, Varna Olympiad 1962.

b) 13...♘b4!? is, in a way, the most critical response to White's idea. If the rook swings over to the kingside the pawn on d4 is left hanging. However, after 14 ♖g3 ♕xd4 15 ♗h6 ♘e8 Black requires great nerves to play this position. Following 16 ♖d1 ♕h4 17 ♗c1 White threatens to win immediately with 18 ♖h3 ♕f6 19 ♖f3 ♕h4 20 ♖f4.

### 14 ♖g3 ♖d8

In his note in *ChessBase Magazine*, the Israeli GM Alexander Huzman gives the line 14...♔h8 15 ♘xd5 exd5 (15...♘xd5 16 ♕g4! ♗f6 17 ♗h6! gxh6 18 ♕g8+! ♖xg8 19 ♘xf7 mate), after which both

sides have an IQP. These pawns are less vulnerable because they are not on half-open files, so they shield each other. In this situation the activity of the pieces is the most significant factor and here White is certainly holding all the trump cards. Huzman continues with 16 ♗g5, with a clear advantage to White – note that 16...♘e4? loses to the tactic 17 ♗xe7 ♕xe7 18 ♗xd5! ♘xg3 19 ♘g6+.

### 15 ♗h6 g6

Or 15...♗f8 16 ♕f3! and White's pressure is already becoming quite unbearable.

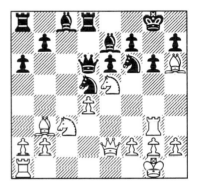

### 16 h4!

Here comes the h-pawn 'battering ram'!

### 16...♗d7 17 h5

Already Black has to be concerned about White crashing through on g6.

### 17...♗e8!

A very useful defensive move, lending indirect support to the g6-pawn and also clearing a piece off the d-file.

The automatic developing move 17...♖ac8 loses after 18 hxg6 hxg6 19 ♘xg6! (naturally) 19...fxg6 20 ♕c2! and Black cannot prevent a disaster occurring around his king, for example 20...♗e8 21 ♖xg6+! ♔h8 22 ♗g7+ ♔g8 23 ♗xf6+.

## 18 ♖d1

White takes a well-earned breather from his kingside offensive in order to lend support to the d4-pawn. Notice that every white piece is performing a useful function.

## 18...♗f8

Black seeks relief with an exchange of bishops.

## 19 hxg6 hxg6

19...♗xh6? 20 gxf7+ regains the piece and leaves Black devoid of defensive pawns.

## 20 ♗g5!

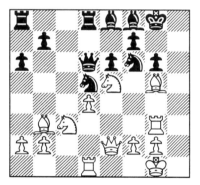

Now the pin on the f6-knight is another cause for concern.

## 20...♖dc8?

20...♗g7 21 ♘xd5 exd5 22 ♖f3 (intending ♕e3-f4 – Huzman) is undoubtedly pleasant for White, but this is still probably Black's best chance of survival.

## 21 ♘e4

21 ♗xf6! ♘xf6 22 d5, combining a kingside attack with the d4-d5 break, looks even more convincing, for example 22...exd5 23 ♘xd5 (threatening ♘xg6 – the bishop on b3 has come to life with a vengeance) 23...♗g7 24 ♘xf6 ♕xf6 25 ♖f3 and White crashes through on f7.

## 21...♘xe4 22 ♕xe4

Now White simply plans to shift queen and rook onto the h-file.

## 22...♗g7

Other moves do not help Black's cause:

a) 22...f6 (this shouldn't work – and it doesn't) 23 ♘xg6! fxg5 (or 23...f5 24 ♗f4! fxe4 25 ♘xf8+ ♔xf8 26 ♗xd6+ ♔f7 27 ♗e5 and Black is lost) 24 ♖xg5 ♗h6 (24...♗g7 25 ♗xd5 exd5 26 ♘e7+ ♔h8 27 ♕e3 and threats of ♖xg7, ♘f5, and ♘xc8 followed by ♕h3+ cannot be parried) 25 ♘e7+ ♔f8 26 ♘xc8 ♖xc8 27 ♖xd5 exd5 28 ♕f5+ and White wins – Huzman.

b) 22...♖c7 23 ♕h4 ♖ac8 24 ♖h3 ♗g7 25 ♕h7+ ♔f8 26 ♖f3 is winning according to Huzman, for example 26...♗xe5 27 dxe5 ♕xe5 28 ♗h6+ ♔e7 29 ♗xd5 exd5 30 ♖e3, winning Black's queen.

## 23 ♕h4 f6

## 24 ♖h3! fxg5

24...fxe5 25 ♕h7+ ♔f8 26 ♖f3+ ♗f7 27 ♗h6 is a killer.

## 25 ♕h7+ ♔f8 26 ♗xd5! g4

Or 26...exd5 27 ♖f3+ ♗f6 28 ♘g4 and Black's position collapses.

## 27 ♘xg4 exd5

27...♕xd5 loses after 28 ♖f3+ ♗f7 29 ♘e5.

28 ♖f3+ ♗f7 29 ♘h6 1-0

29...♖c7 30 ♕g8+ wins everything.

In this next example White shows how a queen swinging to the kingside can also be a powerful attacking idea.

**Belozerov-Perun**
Smolensk 2000
*Caro-Kann Defence*

1 c4 c6 2 e4 d5 3 exd5 cxd5 4 d4 ♘f6 5 ♘c3 e6 6 ♘f3 ♗e7 7 cxd5 ♘xd5 8 ♗d3 ♘c6 9 0-0 0-0 10 ♖e1

Here we have another major theoretical position, which can be reached via the Symmetrical English, the Caro-Kann Defence, the Queen's Gambit Declined, the Scandinavian Defence, or as above.

**10...♗f6**

A logical move, putting immediate pressure on the d4-pawn.

10...♘f6 would transpose to Stoica-Flis above, while 10...b6? is premature here after 11 ♘xd5! and now:

a) 11...♕xd5 12 ♗e4 ♕d6 13 ♘e5 ♗b7 14 ♗f4 ♗f6 15 ♘g6 wins material.

b) 11...exd5 12 ♗xh7+! ♔xh7 13 ♕c2+ wins a pawn.

**11 ♗e4**

This move, adding extra pressure to d5, is White's most popular here. 11 a3, possibly intending ♗c2 and ♕d3, is another approach, although in some ways this justifies 10...♗f6 – Black would follow up with ...g7-g6.

**11...♘ce7**

Supporting the d5-knight and preparing ...♗d7-c6, or ...b7-b6 and ...♗b7.

**12 ♕d3**

Attacking the h7-pawn. White has alternatives here, including 12 ♕b3, putting more pressure on d5, or 12 ♘e5, seizing the e5-outpost now that Black's knight has moved from c6.

**12...h6**

After 12...g6!? 13 ♗h6 Black would have to choose between 13...♗g7, which exchanges a pair of minor pieces but leaves the dark squares around Black's king rather weak, or 13...♖e8.

**13 ♘e5**

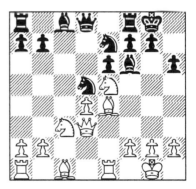

The white knight occupies the e5-outpost and clears the third rank so that the white queen can shift to the kingside – a popular attacking concept in IQP positions. On f3, g3 or h3, the white queen creates annoying threats against Black's kingside structure.

**13...♗d7?**

This natural looking move is a mistake – an indication of how accurately Black has to conduct the defence in certain IQP positions.

Instead Black should exchange a pair of minor pieces with 13...♘xc3 14 ♕xc3 (14 bxc3? ♗xe5 15 dxe5 ♕xd3 16 ♗xd3 ♗d7 gives Black a very pleasant endgame – White kingside initiative is gone and he is left with weaknesses on a2, c3 and e5). Black can continue with 14...♘f5, adding pressure to the d4-pawn: 15 ♗e3 (15 ♗xf5?! exf5 doubles Black's pawns but leaves White vulnerable on the light squares – Black will follow up with ...♗e6-d5 with a more than satisfactory position) 15...a5!? 16 ♖ac1 a4 and Black was okay in Topalov-Karpov, Linares 1995. The Black rook may enter the game via a6.

**14 ♕g3**

Now Black is faced with significant threats.

**14...♔h8?**

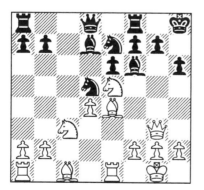

Naturally Black was afraid of ♗xh6 ideas, but after this move he is virtually lost. Black should play 14...♗c6!, after which 15 ♘xc6 bxc6 16 ♗xh6 ♗xd4 17 ♖ad1 ♗f6 is not disastrous for Black, while 15 ♗xh6?! ♘xc3 16 bxc3? ♗xe4

17 ♖xe4 ♘f5! wins material
**15 ♕h3!**

Hitting h6 and, indirectly, d7.

**15...♗xe5**

15...♘xc3 doesn't help Black; after 16 bxc3 White threatens both ♗xb7 and ♗xh6.

**16 ♗xh6!**

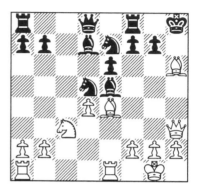

Of course!
**16...f5**

Or 16...♔g8 17 ♗xg7! ♗xh2+ (17...♔xg7 18 ♕h7+ ♔f6 19 dxe5+ ♔xe5 20 ♗xd5+) 18 ♕xh2 ♔xg7 19 ♕h7+ ♔f6 20 ♗xd5 exd5 (20...♘xd5 21 ♘xd5+ exd5 22 ♕h6+ ♔f5 23 ♖e5+ ♔g4 24 ♕g7+ ♕g5 25 ♕xg5 mate) 21 ♕h6+ ♘g6 22 ♘xd5+ ♔f5 23 ♕h5+ ♕g5 24 g4 mate.

**17 ♗g5+ ♔g8 18 ♘xd5! ♗d6**

18...exd5 loses after 19 ♗xd5+ ♘xd5 20 ♗xd8.

**19 ♘xe7+ ♗xe7 20 ♗xe7 ♕xe7 21 ♗xf5**

and White went on to win very comfortably.

The next game, between the two strongest players in the world, is an example of a modern handling of the attack with an IQP.

**Kramnik-Kasparov**
London (6th matchgame) 2000
*Queen's Gambit Accepted*

**1 d4 d5 2 c4 dxc4 3 ♘f3 e6 4 e3 c5 5 ♗xc4 a6 6 0-0 ♘f6 7 a4 ♘c6 8 ♕e2 cxd4 9 ♖d1 ♗e7 10 exd4 0-0 11 ♘c3**

A very well-known position arising from the Queen's Gambit Accepted. White's pieces are again on active squares, but Black also has a positional trumps. Earlier on White played a2-a4 to prevent Black expanding on the queenside with ...b7-b5. This has left Black with an outpost on b4, which may be used by the knight on c6.

**11...♘d5**

Black prevents White from playing an early d4-d5 by simply blocking the pawn. This is a theoretical position which has been assessed in various places as either equal or a slight advantage to White. I was surprised, however, to find that in *Mega Database 2001* Black, with a slightly lower average rating than White, has scored a fine 53% from this position.

11...♘b4, also preventing d4-d5, is Black's main alternative here.

**12 ♗b3**

White has many other moves, including 12 ♕e4 and 12 ♗d3 ♘cb4 13 ♗b1. In the latter variation White's rook on a1 looks entombed, but White can often activate it with the imaginative ♖a3.

**12...♖e8 13 h4!?**

Cutting edge stuff! As we've already seen, h2-h4 is a common way for White to play in an attempt to soften up Black's kingside after ...g7-g6, but playing it this early is a Kramnik-inspired idea. Already quite a few have followed his example.

Alternatives for White include:

a) 13 ♗d2 ♗f6 14 ♕e4 ♘cb4 15 ♘e5 b6 16 ♕f3 ♗b7 17 ♘e4 ♕e7 18 ♖ac1 ♖ac8 and we have a typically unclear position in Gelfand-Ivanchuk, Monaco (rapid) 2000.

b) 13 ♘e5 ♘xc3 14 bxc3 ♘xe5 15 dxe5 ♕c7 16 ♖d3 ♗d7 17 ♖h3 g6 18 ♗h6 ♖ed8 19 ♕e3 ♕c5 20 ♕f4 ♗c6 gives another double-edged position in Naumkin-Sadler, Ostend 1992.

**13...♘cb4**

In his notes in *Informator* Kramnik gives the continuation 13...♗xh4 14 ♘xh4 ♘xc3 15 bxc3 ♕xh4 16 d5 ♘a5 17 ♗c2, when White has good compensation for the pawn.

**14 h5**

Kramnik continues the charge. The h-pawn will be pushed to h6, thus inducing Black to make some sort of permanent weakness in his kingside. This plan is quite double-edged, as the pawn itself on h6 can become a weakness, as well as a thorn in Black's side.

**14...b6 15 ♘e5**

A more recent example is 15 ♗d2 ♗b7 16 h6 g6 17 ♘e4 a5 18 ♗c4 f6 19 ♖ac1 ♗c6 20 b3 ♕d7 21 ♖e1 ♔h8 22 ♘h2 ♘a2 23 ♖cd1 ♘ab4 24 ♘g4 ♗d8? 25 ♗xb4 axb4 26 ♕f3 ♕f7? (26...f5 27 ♘e5 fxe4 28 ♖xe4 ♕c7 29 ♘xc6 ♕xc6 30 ♗b5 wins) 27 ♘d6 1-0 Stefansson-Izoria, European Championship, Ohrid 2001.

**15...♗b7 16 a5!**

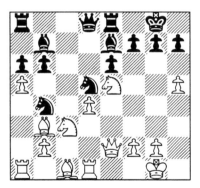

**16...b5!?**

A risky decision, as now White has access to the c5-square as an outpost. 16...bxa5? 17 ♗a4 ♖f8 18 h6 g6 19 ♘d7 ♖e8 20 ♕e5 ♘f6 21 ♘c5 ♗c6 22 ♘xe6! is good for White, but 16...♖c8!? may be Black's best move.

**17 h6 g6 18 ♘e4 ♘c7?**

This unforced retreat is a definite mistake. The natural 18...♖c8! is stronger.

**19 ♘c5?!**

19 ♗d2! ♗d5 (19...♕xd4 20 ♘g5,

gives White a powerful attack) 20 ♗xd5 ♘cxd5 21 ♖ac1 gives White a clear advantage according to Kramnik.

**19...♗d5 20 ♖a3!? ♘c6! 21 ♗xd5**

21 ♘xc6!? ♗xc6 22 ♗c2 keeps an edge according to the Slovakian grandmaster Lubomir Ftacnik.

**21...♕xd5 22 ♘cd7 ♖ad8!**

Kasparov shows defensive ingenuity. 22...♘xd4? 23 ♕g4 wins the pinned knight on d4, while 22...f6 23 ♖ad3! fxe5 24 dxe5 ♕c4 (or 24...♕a2 25 ♖c3) 25 ♘b6 is very good for White.

**23 ♘xc6 ♖xd7 24 ♘xe7+ ♖exe7 25 ♖c3 f6 26 ♗e3 ♔f7**

Black has managed to simplify, but White still has control of the c5-square and the c-file, while h6 could yet prove to be either a strength or a weakness.

**27 ♖dc1 ♕b7 28 ♖c5 ♘d5 29 ♕f3 ♘b4! 30 ♕e2 ♖c7!?**

Perhaps the match situation of being a game down persuades Kasparov to play for a win. Objectively Black should repeat with 30...♘d5.

**31 ♗f4 ♖xc5 32 dxc5 e5 33 ♕d2!**

White's passed pawn on c5 gives him the better chances. We've moved a little away from an IQP position, so I'll give the rest of the game with just light notes.

**33...♞c6 34 ♕d5+ ♚f8 35 ♗e3 ♕d7 36 ♕f3 ♚f7 37 ♖d1 e4! 38 ♕e2 ♕f5 39 ♖d6 ♖e6 40 ♖d7+ ♖e7 41 ♖d6 ♖e6 42 ♕d1 g5?**

42...♖xd6 43 ♕xd6 ♕e6 44 ♕c7+ ♞e7 45 ♗d4 ♕d5 is equal – Kramnik.

**43 ♕h5+? ♚e7 44 ♕d1 ♚f7?**

44...♚e8! 45 ♖d7 ♖e7 46 ♖xe7+ ♞xe7 47 ♕d6 ♕d7.

**45 ♖d7+!**

Now Kramnik hits upon the right idea.

**45...♚g6**

Or:

a) 45...♖e7? 46 ♕b3+ ♚f8 47 ♖d6 ♖c7 48 ♗d4 ♞xd4 49 ♖d8+ ♚e7 50 ♕g8 ♞e2+ 51 ♚f1 ♞g3+ 52 ♚e1 and White is winning.

b) 45...♞e7 46 c6! ♖xc6 47 ♕h5+ ♕g6 48 ♕xg6+ hxg6 49 h7 ♖c8 50 ♗c5 and the knight on e7 is lost.

**46 ♖g7+ ♚xh6 47 ♕d7 ♖e5**

47...♞e5 48 ♖xh7+! ♕xh7 49 ♕xe6 ♚g6 50 ♕xa6 ♕h5 51 ♕xb5 and White's three passed pawns on the queenside will decide the issue.

**48 ♕f7**

Now Black is in virtual zugzwang.

**48...♖d5 49 ♚h1**

49 b4! wins after 49...♞xb4 (49...♞e5 50 ♗xg5+ fxg5 51 ♕xf5 ♞f3+ 52 gxf3

♖xf5 53 ♖a7) 50 ♚h2 ♞c6 51 g4!.

**49...♞d8 50 ♖xh7+ ♕xh7 51 ♕xd5 ♚g6+ 52 ♚g1 ♕c7 53 ♕g8+ ♚f5 54 ♕d5+ ♚g6 55 ♕xe4+ ♚g7 56 ♕a8?**

In a hurry to win the a6-pawn, Kramnik creates problems for himself. 56 ♕d5! ♞c6 57 ♗d4 ♚g6 58 ♗c3 gives White a decisive advantage – Ftacnik.

**56...♕d7**

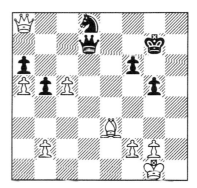

**57 ♚h2?**

White still retains some winning chances after 57 f3.

**57...♕d3 58 g3**

Or 58 ♕xa6 ♕h7+ 59 ♚g3 ♕h4+ 60 ♚f3 f5 and suddenly Black has counterplay against the white king.

**58...♞f7 59 ♕b7 ♚g6 60 ♕xa6 ♞e5 61 ♕a8 ♞g4+ 62 ♚h3 ♕f5!**

Kasparov's counter-attack is assuming dangerous proportions, so much so that Kramnik now decides to bail out by giving perpetual check.

**63 ♕g8+**

Or 63 ♚g2 ♞xe3+ 64 fxe3 ♕c2+ 65 ♚f1 (but not 65 ♚h3?? g4+! 66 ♚xg4 ♕f5+ 67 ♚h4 ♕h5 mate) 65...♕d1 and it's Black who gives perpetual check.

**63...♚h6 64 ♕h8+ ♚g6 65 ♕e8+ ♚h6 66 ♕h8+ ½-½**

**Seger-Emms**
German Bundesliga 2000
*Sicilian Defence*

1 e4 c5 2 c3 d5 3 exd5 ♕xd5 4 d4
♘f6 5 ♘f3 ♘c6 6 ♗e3 cxd4 7 cxd4
e6 8 ♘c3 ♕d6 9 a3 ♗e7 10 ♗d3 b6
11 0-0 0-0 12 ♕e2 ♗b7 13 ♖ad1

Here it could be said that both sides can be content with their positions. White has developed normally and can continue to add pressure with moves such as ♖fe1, ♗g5, and then ♗c4 (lining up d4-d5) or ♗b1 and ♕c2 (eyeing h7). Notice that earlier in the game White played a2-a3, a useful move which prevents ...♘b4. For his part Black has developed his pieces and has some pressure on the d4-pawn. He is ready to bring his rooks into the game and can contemplate blocking the d4-pawn with ...♘f6-d5. Initially Black's play is generally a reaction to White's threats, but there are also certain favourable manoeuvres for Black and he will always be on the lookout for agreeable exchanges. Theoretically speaking White has a small advantage here. In *Mega Database 2001* White scores 54% (this is average).

**13...♖fd8**

A sensible move, adding more pressure to the d4-pawn. This feels like the right rook, as the other one has a nice square on c8. Alternatively:

a) Black can block the pawn with 13...♘d5!?, but the flip side is that this leaves him without his defensive knight on f6. 14 ♘xd5 ♕xd5 15 ♗c4 ♕h5 16 d5 ♘a5! is unclear, but White can keep an edge by keeping the pieces on with 14 ♘e4.

b) 13...♖fe8 14 ♖fe1 g6 (Black plans ...♗f8-g7 in order to bolster his kingside and add extra indirect pressure on the d4-pawn) 15 ♗g5 ♘d5 16 ♘e4 ♕c7 17 h4! (now ...♗xg5 is met by hxg5 and the g5-pawn is a pain for Black) 17...f5?! (Black must think very carefully before creating a weakness like this; 17...♘f4 18 ♕e3 ♘xd3 19 ♖xd3 leaves Black with weak dark squares around his king, but 17...♗f8!?, planning ...♗g7, looks okay) 18 ♘c3 ♗xg5 19 hxg5 ♘f4 20 ♕e3 ♘xd3 21 ♕xd3 ♕f4? 22 d5!. This d4-d5 break comes with a great advantage for White in Emms-Pedersen, Drury Lane 1997 – 22...exd5 23 ♘xd5 and ♘f6+ is coming.

**14 ♖fe1**

At first sight this may look a little strange, as the rook's effect is blocked by the bishop on e3. However, the e3-square is rather a passive place for this bishop. It will eventually move away, allowing the queen and rook to bear down the e-file. Then White can think about a d4-d5 breakthrough or, more ambitiously, piece sacrifices on e6 and f7.

**14...♖ac8**

Black now has all of his pieces on relatively good squares and is ready to counter White's offensives.

**15 ♗g5**

With this move White unleashes his queen and rook down the half-open e-file and adds pressure to the d5-square by attacking one of its defenders. White does, however, have a couple of important alternatives.

a) 15 ♗c1 (The idea of moving the bishop back to its home square needs some digestion, but it all makes perfect sense. White can continue with ♗b1 and unleash the major piece power down the d- and e-files.) 15...h6!? (A relatively new idea: instead of passively waiting Black intends to re-route his dark squared bishop to g7 after ...g7-g6 and ...♗f8-g7. From here the bishop protects the kingside and adds more pressure to the d4-pawn. An immediate 15...♗f8 would be met by an annoying 16 ♗g5, hence the need for 15...h6. It's a slightly risky plan, as Black is moving pawns in front of his own king.) 16 ♗b1 ♗f8 17 ♘e4 ♘xe4 (17...♕e7!?) 18 ♕xe4 g6 19 ♕h4 (eyeing the pawn on h6) 19...♕e7 20 ♕h3! (20 ♕xe7?! ♘xe7 would be a terrible decision from White – suddenly the actual static weakness of the d4-pawn becomes the most important aspect of the position) 20...♕f6 21 d5 (21 ♗xh6 ♗xh6 22

♕xh6 ♘xd4 23 ♘xd4 ♖xd4 24 ♖xd4 ♕xd4 is okay for Black) 21...♖xd5 22 ♖xd5 exd5 23 ♗xh6 ♗xh6 24 ♕xh6

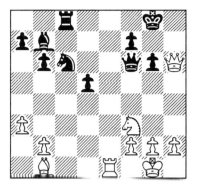

with an unclear position in Rozentalis-Andersson, Tilburg 1993.

b) 15 ♗b1!? (this is very direct – White plans ♕c2 followed by some tactics involving d4-d5) 15...h6 16 ♕c2. White's position is beginning to look really threatening, but Black can defend with a cool head:

b1) 16...♗f8? (Black needs one more move with ...g7-g6, but there is not enough time) 17 d5 exd5 18 ♘xd5 and Black is in some trouble as 18...♘xd5 allows mate with 19 ♕h7.

b2) 16...♘a5!? (unleashing the power of the bishop on b7 and the rook on c8; d4-d5 has been well and truly prevented – at least for the moment. On the other hand this knight no longer protects e5 so...) 17 ♘e5 ♗d5!? (17...♘c4 18 ♗f4! ♘xe5 19 ♗xe5 ♕c6 20 d5! is good for White) 18 ♘g4 ♔f8! (prophylaxis – it turns out that allowing the white queen to h7 isn't a disaster after all) 19 ♘xf6 ♗xf6 20 ♕h7 ♘c4 21 ♗e4 (21 ♗f4? ♕xf4 22 ♘xd5 ♖xd5 23 ♕h8+ ♔e7 24 ♕xc8 ♗xd4 is good for Black – 25 ♖f1 ♗xf2+! 26 ♔h1 ♕xh2+!! and it's mate next move) 21...♘xe3 22 fxe3 ♗b3 23 ♗c2 ♗xc2 24 ♕xc2 ♔g8 and Black was fine in Segal-Peptan, Yerevan Women's Olympiad 1996.

**15...h6**

Putting the question to the bishop. Other moves include:

a) 15...♘d5? (trying to exchange pieces, but the tactics don't work for Black here) 16 ♘xd5 ♕xd5 17 ♗e4 ♕d7 18 d5! (another successful d4-d5 break) 18...exd5 19 ♖xd5 and Black loses in every line, for example 19...♕g4 20 ♗xe7 ♘xe7 21 ♖xd8+ ♖xd8 22 ♗xb7, 19...♕e8 20 ♖xd8 ♕xd8 21 ♗xc6, or 19...♕e6 20 ♖xd8+ ♗xd8 (20...♖xd8 21 ♗xc6 ♕xe2 22 ♖xe2 ♗xg5 23 ♗xb7) 21 ♕d3.

b) 15...♘a5 uncovers the light-squared bishop and the c8-rook, but more importantly it allows White to grab the e5-outpost with 16 ♘e5!. After this Black must proceed with great care, for example 16...♘c6? runs into 17 ♗xf6 ♗xf6 18 ♗xh7+! ♔xh7 19 ♕h5+ ♔g8 20 ♕xf7+ ♔h7 21 ♖d3! with a winning attack, while 16...♘d5 17 ♗xh7+! ♔xh7 18 ♕h5+ ♔g8 19 ♕xf7+ ♔h7 20 ♖d3 is also winning for White – 20...♗xg5 21 ♖h3+ ♗h6 22 ♖xh6+ ♔xh6 23 ♕g6 is mate.

c) 15...g6, killing the threat against h7, is a sensible alternative. White should probably play 16 ♗c4, moving to the other diagonal and planning d4-d5. After 16...♘a5 17 ♗a2 White keeps an edge.

**16 ♗xf6**

16 ♗c1 leaves White a tempo down over 15 ♗c1. Black continues with 16...♗f8 17 ♗b1 g6 and will follow up with ...♗g7

16 ♗h4 keeps the tension. Now

16...♘xd4? loses material after 17 ♘xd4 ♕xd4 18 ♗e4!, but after 16...♕f4! 17 ♗g3 ♕g4 18 h3 ♕h5 Black's queen is reasonably well placed on h5.

**16...♗xf6 17 d5**

The logical follow-up to White's earlier play. The desirable d4-d5 break is achieved with the support of White's remaining pieces. On this occasion, however, Black has enough resources in his position to equalise.

**17...♘d4!**

This shot, which had to be calculated before playing 15...h6, allows Black to enter a reasonable ending.

17...exd5 18 ♘xd5 gives Black more problems, for example 18...♕xd5? 19 ♗h7+ ♔xh7 20 ♖xd5 ♖xd5 21 ♕e4+!, or 18...♘d4? 19 ♘xf6+ ♕xf6 20 ♘xd4 ♖xd4 21 ♕e8+!. Notice how the value of having rooks on e1 and d1 is apparent in this final line.

**18 ♘xd4 ♗xd4 19 dxe6**

19 ♕e4?! looks promising, but after 19...♗xc3 20 ♕h7+ ♔f8 21 bxc3 (21 dxe6 ♗xe1 22 e7+ ♔xe7 23 ♖xe1+ ♔d7 24 ♗f5+ ♔c7 wins for Black) 21...♕xd5 22 ♕h8+ ♔e7 23 ♕xg7 ♖g8! it's Black who has the killing counterattack.

**19...♕xe6 20 ♕xe6 fxe6**

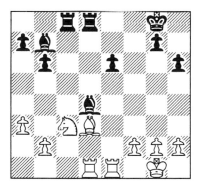

The position is roughly level – Black has the bishop pair in an open position but this advantage is offset by the weak e6-pawn. The game concluded **21 ♘b5!** (21 ♖xe6 ♗xc3 22 bxc3 ♖xc3 23 ♖e3 ♔f8 is better for Black – the a3-pawn is vulnerable) **21...♗xb2 22 ♘xa7 ♖a8 23 ♘b5 ♗d5 24 ♘c7 ♖xa3 25 ♗e4 ♖f8 26 ♘xd5 ½-½**

### Attacking Against the IQP

The last few examples may be enough to put off anyone facing an IQP, but I have to stress that in some of the cases above White started with a significant theoretical advantage (Black was entering into dodgy opening variations). There are plenty of openings involving White having the IQP where Black, if he plays correctly, can neutralise White's initiative and then hope to exploit the weakness of the IQP later in the game. The next two examples are cases of this.

### Korchnoi-Karpov
Merano (9th matchgame) 1981
*Queen's Gambit Declined*

**1 c4 e6 2 ♘c3 d5 3 d4 ♗e7 4 ♘f3 ♘f6 5 ♗g5 h6 6 ♗h4 0-0 7 ♖c1 dxc4 8 e3 c5 9 ♗xc4 cxd4 10 exd4**

More recently players have been turning their attention towards 10 ♘xd4 – an indication that this particular IQP position doesn't hold too many fears for the black player.

**10...♘c6 11 0-0**

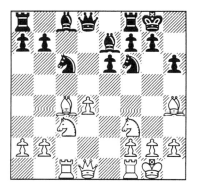

**11...♘h5!**

A good simplifying procedure – Black ensures that a pair of minor pieces are exchanged. In this respect the early insertion of the moves ...h7-h6 and ♗h4 has been very useful for Black.

Another possible idea is to attack the d-pawn immediately with 11...♕b6 and ...♖fd8. White should probably combat this idea with ♕d2 and ♖fd1.

**12 ♗xe7**

12 ♗g3?! ♘xg3 13 hxg3 ♗f6 promises Black at least equality. White has immediate problems with his d-pawn – 14 d5 is met by 14...♘a5.

**12...♘xe7**

An exchange of a pair of minor pieces has helped Black. It's true that the knight on h5 is offside, but this is soon brought back into the game.

**13 ♗b3?!**

This looks rather aimless – White must play actively. After 13 ♖e1! Black must play more accurately, for example 13...♘f6 14 ♘e5 and now:

a) 14...♗d7 15 ♕b3 ♖b8 (Christiansen-Karpov, London 1982) 16 ♘xd7! ♘xd7 (16...♕xd7 17 ♖xe6!) 17 d5 exd5 18 ♘xd5 ♘xd5 19 ♗xd5 is better for White – the bishop is superior to the knight in this open position.

b) 14...♕b6! 15 ♖c2 ♖d8 16 ♖d2 ♗d7 17 ♗b3 ♗e8! with an equal position in Piket-Van der Sterren, Dutch Championship 1993.

**13...♘f6 14 ♘e5 ♗d7**

Planning to put the bishop on the long diagonal after ...♗c8 and ...♗c6. 14...b6 is a slightly riskier way to develop the bishop here, but is possible after 15 ♕f3 ♗a6 16 ♖fd1 ♖c8.

**15 ♕e2 ♖c8**

**16 ♘e4?**

A very strange decision from Korchnoi. White gains nothing from this exchange – as pieces are exchanged the weakness of the isolated pawn becomes more and more apparent.

**16...♘xe4 17 ♕xe4 ♗c6! 18 ♘xc6 ♖xc6!**

18...♘xc6? 19 d5 allows White to get rid of his weakness.

**19 ♖c3**

After 19 ♖xc6 Black has two possible recaptures:

a) 19...♘xc6? allows White to liquidate his weakness with 20 d5. After 20...exd5 21 ♗xd5 it's White who's better – he has bishop versus knight in an open position.

b) 19...bxc6! is the correct recapture. Black accepts an isolated c-pawn, but on this occasion d4 is much more difficult to defend than c6. Black will continue with ...♕b6 and ...♖d8, while the knight on e7 does a good job defending c6. Nevertheless, White should probably go in for this. He can play 20 ♖c1 with the idea of ♖c4; here the rook both attacks c6 and defends d4.

**19...♕d6 20 g3 ♖d8 21 ♖d1 ♖b6!**

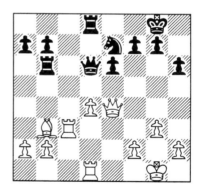

With ideas of ...♖b4.

**22 ♕e1**

22 ♗c2 g6 easily deals with the threat of ♕h7+ and leaves White wondering what to do about his b-pawn.

**22...♕d7 23 ♖cd3 ♖d6 24 ♕e4 ♕c6 25 ♕f4**

25 ♕xc6 loses a pawn after 25...♘xc6 26 d5 ♘b4!.

**25...♘d5 26 ♕d2 ♕b6**

White has been driven to total passivity and Black now threatens ...♘b4. This threat should be dealt with by 27 a3.

**27 ♗xd5? ♖xd5**

A very grim IQP position for White! Irish GM Alex Baburin points out in *Winning Pawn Structures* that the IQP is very difficult to defend in pure major piece endings such as this. Black's basic plan is to now treble on the d-file and then play ...e6-e5. This can only be prevented by f2-f4, but this adds a crucial second weakness to White's position. Karpov's technique from here on in is quite immaculate.

**28 ♖b3 ♕c6 29 ♕c3 ♕d7 30 f4**

Or else ...e6-e5 is coming.

**30...b6 31 ♖b4 b5!**

Threatening ...a7-a5.

**32 a4 bxa4 33 ♕a3 a5! 34 ♖xa4 ♕b5!**

The weakness created by f2-f4 is starting to cause White headaches. He has to be wary of infiltration with ...♕e2 and possibly ...♖h5. And all the time, that d-pawn still needs constant protection.

**35 ♖d2 e5!**

Starting an all-out assault on the white king.

**36 fxe5 ♖xe5**

Threatening ...♖e1+.

**37 ♕a1 ♕e8**

Again threatening ...♖e1+. Karpov has

traded advantages very efficiently.

**38 dxe5 ♖xd2 39 ♖xa5**

Or 39 ♕e1 ♕d7 40 ♖a1 ♕d4+ 41 ♔f1 ♖xh2 and Black cleans up.

**39...♕c6**

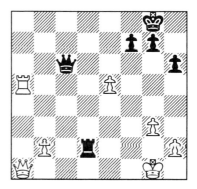

**40 ♖a8+ ♔h7 41 ♕b1+ g6 42 ♕f1 ♕c5+**

There's still time to waste all the previous good work: 42...♕xa8?? allows White to escape with a draw after 43 ♕xf7+ ♔h8 44 ♕f6+ ♔h7 (44...♔g8?? 45 ♕xg6+ ♔f8 46 ♕xh6+ and it's White who wins) 45 ♕f7+, with perpetual check.

**43 ♔h1 ♕d5+ 0-1**

44...♖d1 will follow. An altogether impressive demonstration by Karpov, although it has to be said that Korchnoi was very accommodating on this particular occasion.

**Buckley-Emms**
British Championship 2000
*Nimzo-Indian Defence*

**1 d4 ♘f6 2 c4 e6 3 ♘c3 ♗b4 4 ♘f3 c5 5 e3 0-0 6 ♗d3 d5 7 0-0 cxd4 8 exd4 dxc4 9 ♗xc4 b6**

This line of the Nimzo-Indian is a favourite of Anatoly Karpov, who, as we have already seen, has a liking for facing the IQP.

**10 ♗g5 ♗b7 11 ♖c1 ♘c6 12 a3 ♗e7 13 ♖e1**

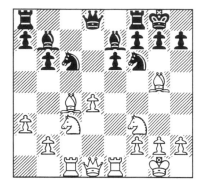

Another characteristic IQP position. I would consider this theoretical position to be very slightly in White's favour, although I would also agree that it's also a matter of taste – some would prefer the IQP, some would prefer to play against it, some would like to play either side and some wouldn't want to play either side!

Here Black attempts to use tactics in order to exchange pieces and thus nullify White's initiative.

**13...♘d5!?**

Blocking the passed pawn and offering an exchange of minor pieces. Black could also consider 13...♖c8!?, and if 14 ♗a2 only then 14...♘d5.

**14 ♗xd5**

I prefer 14 ♗d2! ♘xc3 15 ♗xc3 ♗f6 16 d5! (otherwise Black plays ...♘e7!) 16...♗xc3 17 ♖xc3 exd5 18 ♗xd5 and the simplified position is slightly in White's favour.

**14...♗xg5!**

Now the placing of the rook on c1 proves to be a little unfortunate for

White. As it's attacked by the bishop on g5, Black forces further exchanges which frees his position.

14...exd5?! would be an error. The pawn structure changes in White's favour, with an isolated pair on d4 and d5. Following 15 ♗xe7 ♘xe7, White's pawn on d4 is no longer easy to attack, plus black's bishop on b7 is blocked by its own pawn on d5.

**15 ♘xg5 ♕xg5**

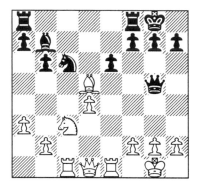

**16 ♗f3?!**

Given the exchange of two sets of minor pieces, it's already time for White to be thinking about obtaining by exchanging his isolated pawn. 16 ♗e4 ♖fd8 17 d5 exd5 18 ♘xd5 looks like a good way to do this.

**16...♖fd8!**

Now Black already has a slight advantage, Two pairs of minor pieces have been exchanged and White cannot simplify with d4-d5. The pin on the long diagonal is of no significance here.

**17 ♘e2**

17 d5 ♘e5! 18 ♗e4 exd5 19 ♘xd5 ♘g6 gives White problems with the pinned knight on the d-file.

**17...♖ac8 18 b4?**

This overly aggressive move causes

significant problems later on. White isn't allowed to play a favourable b4-b5 and the c3-square is now irrevocably weakened – this second weakness proves to be vitally important.

18 ♕a4? loses material to the tactic 18...♘xd4!, so best is 18 ♖c2, planning ♖d2.

**18...h6 19 ♖c2 ♕e7**

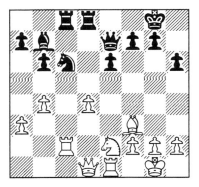

With this move Black defends the bishop on b7 and plans to put extra pressure on the d-pawn with ...♕d7.

**20 ♖d2**

20 b5 doesn't work: 20...♘xd4! 21 ♘xd4 ♖xc2 22 ♕xc2 ♖xd4 leaves Black a pawn up.

**20...♕d7 21 ♘f4**

Once again 21 d5 fails to 21...♘c5!.

**21...♘e7**

Taking no chances with White's d4-pawn – it won't run away. 21...♘xd4? loses material to 22 ♗xb7 ♕xb7 23 ♖xd4, while 21...♗a8 threatens ...♘xd4, but allows 22 d5 when 22...♘e7 23 d6 ♗xf3 24 ♕xf3 ♘f5 25 ♖ed1 is unclear.

**22 ♗g4**

Threatening ♘xe6, but this is easily countered. Notice that White now has to watch out for ...♖c3 – a direct consequence of White's faulty 18th move.

**22...♗d5**

Blocking the d-pawn and stopping all tricks on e6. It's true that the pressure on the d4-pawn is temporarily released, but now Black has control of the c-file.

**23 ♘d3 ♕b7 24 ♘e5**

Now 24...♗xg2? 25 ♘xf7! ♔xf7 26 ♗xe6+ ♔f8 27 ♕g4! is good for White; Black still must be careful to keep control.

**24...♖c3!**

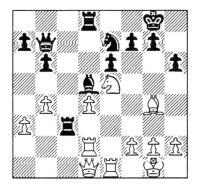

How White wishes that pawn was back on b2!

**25 ♖d3 ♖dc8 26 ♕d2 ♖xd3 27 ♕xd3 ♕c7 28 ♖d1**

28 ♗h5 is effectively met by 28...g6, as 29 ♗xg6? doesn't work after 29...fxg6 30 ♘xg6 ♘xg6 31 ♕xg6+ ♕g7.

**28...♕c3**

There is no need for Black to fear an exchange of queens – in fact this is positively encouraged. Vulnerable white pawns and control of the c-file give Black excellent chances of victory in an ending

**29 ♕a6 ♖c7 30 ♕b5 ♘c6 31 ♗f3?**

31 ♕d3 loses a pawn after 31...♘xe5 32 ♕xc3 ♖xc3 33 dxe5 ♖xa3. White's best chance of hanging on is with 31 ♘xc6 ♖xc6 – Black is in total command,

but has no immediate way to win material.

**31...♗xf3 32 gxf3**

32 ♘xf3 ♕xa3 33 d5 ♕xb4 34 ♕xb4 ♘xb4 35 d6 ♖d7 36 ♘e5 ♖d8 37 ♔f1 ♘d5 38 d7 f6 leaves Black with a winning ending.

**32...♘xe5 33 ♕xe5**

Or 33 dxe5 ♕xf3 34 ♕e8+ ♔h7 35 ♖d8 ♖c1+.

**33...♖c8**

Now White is losing at least a pawn – there is no good way of defending all the weaknesses.

**34 f4**

34 ♕e3 ♕xe3 35 fxe3 ♖c3 should be a winning rook and pawn ending for Black.

**34...♕xa3 35 ♔g2 ♕xb4 36 f5 ♕c4 37 ♖a1 a5 38 ♖b1 ♕d5+?!**

This is sufficient but 38...♖c6 is an easier route to victory

**39 ♕xd5 exd5 40 ♖xb6 ♖a8!**

The rook is well posted, supporting the passed pawn from behind. White's rook is forced into passivity.

**41 ♔f3 a4 42 ♔f4 a3 43 ♖b1 a2 44 ♖a1 f6 45 ♔g4 ♔f7 46 ♔h5 ♖a7 47 f4 ♔e7 48 ♔g6 ♔d6 49 h4 ♔c6 50 h5 ♔b5 51 ♖xa2**

Or else ...♔c4-b3.

**51...♖xa2 52 ♔xg7 ♔c4 53 ♔xf6 ♔xd4 54 ♔g7 ♖g2+ 55 ♔xh6 ♔c5!**
**0-1**

Of course, having that extra tempo with the white pieces certainly helps. In the following two games, it's Black who accepts the IQP and in both cases he is quickly forced onto the defensive.

**Benko-Ostojic**
Sao Paulo 1973
*Queen's Gambit Declined*

**1 d4 ♘f6 2 c4 e6 3 ♘f3 c5 4 e3 d5 5 ♘c3 ♘c6 6 a3 a6 7 dxc5 ♗xc5 8 b4**

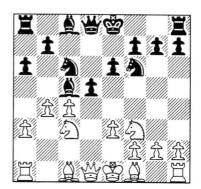

**8...♗e7?!**

The bishop is not particularly well placed on e7 in the upcoming IQP position – its activity is rather limited.

8...♗d6 is stronger, but Black's main move is 8...♗a7. Then after 9 ♗b2 0-0 10 cxd5 exd5 the bishop is well placed for a ...d5-d4 breakthrough. For example 11 ♗e2 ♖e8!? (11...d4 12 exd4 ♘xd4 13 ♘xd4 ♗xd4 leads to immediate equality; 11...♖e8 is more ambitious) 12 0-0 ♕d6 13 ♕c2 ♗g4 14 h3 ♗h5 15 ♖fd1 ♖ad8

16 ♖d2?! ♗b8 17 g3? ♖xe3! 18 ♔g2 d4 19 ♖ad1 ♗xf3+ 20 ♗xf3 d3 21 ♕b1 ♖xf3 22 ♔xf3 ♘e5+ 23 ♔g2 ♕c6+ 24 f3 ♕xf3+ and White resigned in Acosta-Tempone, Mar del Plata 1997 – another good advert for the IQP, although White's play was decidedly dodgy. It should be said that theory prefers 10 ♕c2 instead of 10 cxd5, which is an indication that the IQP position is fine for Black after 10 cxd5.

**9 ♗b2 0-0 10 cxd5 exd5 11 ♗e2 ♖e8 12 0-0**

The extra tempo gained by having the white pieces, coupled with Black's dubious 8th move, gives White a clear edge here. Black will have to be more concerned about his defensive duties regarding the IQP, at least for the moment, rather than any active operations.

**11...♗g4 13 h3 ♗h5?!**

Black's position just isn't strong enough to justify the bishop being here. The IQP needs some support, so 13...♗e6! is critical.

**14 ♕b3!**

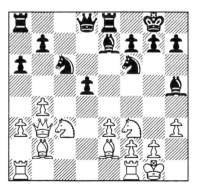

White turns to active harassment of the IQP; ♖ad1 (or ♖fd1) will give Black plenty of problems.

**14...♕d7**

Black already has big problems, as the following variations demonstrate:

a) 14...♗xf3 15 ♗xf3 d4 16 ♖fd1 ♘e5 17 ♗xb7 ♖a7 18 exd4.

b) 14...d4 15 ♖ad1.

c) 14...♕d6 15 ♖ad1 ♖ad8 and White can choose between 16 ♖d2 and 16 g4 ♗g6 17 g5 ♘e4 18 ♘xd5.

**15 ♖ad1 ♖ad8 16 ♘a4!**

Unleashing the bishop along the long diagonal and also producing the idea of ♘b6. White wins the d5-pawn by force.

**16...♕e6**

16...♘e4 17 ♘b6 picks up the d5-pawn.

**17 ♗xf6 ♗xf6 18 ♘c5 ♕e7 19 ♖xd5 ♖xd5 20 ♕xd5**

and White is a healthy pawn to the good.

**Karpov-Kasparov**
Moscow (9th matchgame 1984)
*Queen's Gambit Declined*

**1 d4 d5 2 c4 e6 3 ♘f3 c5 4 cxd5 exd5 5 g3 ♘f6 6 ♗g2 ♗e7 7 0-0 0-0 8 ♘c3 ♘c6 9 ♗g5 cxd4 10 ♘xd4 h6 11 ♗e3 ♖e8**

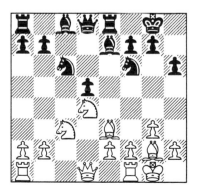

A promising IQP position for White. The d-pawn is blocked by the knight on d4 and attacked by the c3-knight. Another attacker is White's light-squared bishop, which is very well placed on g2, both attacking the d5-pawn and defending the king.

It's not all doom and gloom for Black; his pieces are reasonably active. However, theory gives this position as slightly better for White and in practice White's results have been good (White has scored 62% in *Mega Database 2001*).

**12 ♕b3**

Putting more pressure on the d5-pawn and virtually forcing Black's next move.

**12...♞a5 13 ♕c2 ♗g4 14 ♞f5 ♖c8 15 ♗d4**

White's dark-squared bishop is very well placed on d4, blocking the IQP and pointing towards both the kingside and the queenside. Given that, it's unsurprising that Kasparov now offers to exchange bishops. As we've already seen before, though, exchanges often help the player battling against the IQP.

**15...♗c5 16 ♗xc5 ♖xc5 17 ♞e3!**

On this occasion attacking the d5-pawn directly is better than blocking it. After 17 ♞d4 ♞e4! 18 e3 ♞xc3 19 bxc3 ♕c7 White has a weakness of his own.

**17...♗e6**

17...d4 is effectively met by 18 ♖ad1.

**18 ♖ad1 ♕c8 19 ♕a4 ♖d8 20 ♖d3**

White slowly builds up the pressure on the IQP. ♖fd1 is the idea.

**20...a6 21 ♖fd1 ♞c4**

Black uses tactics in order to exchange his offside knight.

**22 ♞xc4**

22 ♞exd5 allows Black to simplify into an equal ending after 22...♞xd5 23 ♞xd5 ♗xd5 24 ♗xd5 ♖dxd5! 25 ♖xd5 ♖xd5 26 ♖xd5 ♞b6 27 ♕d4 ♞xd5 28 ♕xd5 ♕c1+ 29 ♔g2 ♕xb2.

**22...♖xc4 23 ♕a5 ♖c5 24 ♕b6 ♖d7 25 ♖d4 ♕c7**

More often than not exchanges help the player fighting against the IQP, but that is only a general rule. In this particular position it eases Black defensive burden by offering to exchange off White's active queen.

**26 ♕xc7 ♖dxc7 27 h3**

Preparing g3-g4, gaining space on the kingside. Kasparov prevents this with his next move.

Black has defended well and White has only a small advantage going into the ending. He also has to be careful not to let this slip. 27 ♞xd5?! allows Black the opportunity to simplify into a drawn rook and pawn ending after 27...♘xd5 28 ♗xd5 ♗xd5 29 ♖xd5 ♖xd5 30 ♖xd5 ♖c2, for example 31 ♖d8+ ♔h7 32 ♖d7 ♖xb2 33 ♖xf7 ♖xe2 – Karpov.

**27...h5 28 a3 g6 29 e3 ♔g7 30 ♔h2 ♖c4 31 ♗f3 b5 32 ♔g2**

Defending the f2-pawn and bringing the king towards the centre.

**32...♖7c5 33 ♖xc4 ♖xc4!?**

33...dxc4? rids Black of the IQP, but after 34 ♖d6 a5 35 ♖b6 Black loses a pawn – 35...♗d7 loses to 36 ♖xf6!.

33...bxc4!? is possible, but Black still has problems over his d5-pawn.

Black is quite happy to give up his d-pawn in order to reach a theoretically drawn ending. After 34 ♘xd5?! ♘xd5 35 ♗xd5 ♗xd5+ 36 ♖xd5 ♖c2 37 ♖d6 ♖xb2 38 ♖xa6 b4! the queenside pawns are exchanged and the 4v3 pawn majority on the kingside offers only very small practical winning chances. At this level the result would almost certainly be a draw.

**34 ♖d4!?**

An interesting decision. Karpov offers the exchange of rooks and is prepared to take on an isolated pawn himself. However, after an exchange on d4 White will still retain an edge – the d5-pawn will be more vulnerable than its counterpart on d4 and White's bishop is superior to Black's.

**34...♔f8 35 ♗e2**

Forcing the issue.

**35...♖xd4 36 exd4 ♔e7 37 ♘a2**

Eyeing the c5-outpost, via b4 and d3.

**37...♗c8 38 ♘b4 ♔d6 39 f3**

Eliminating the possibility of ...♘e4 and preparing to centralise the king with ♔f2-e3.

**39...♘g8**

A useful manoeuvre. The knight wants to go to f5, where it attacks the d4-pawn.

**40 h4 ♘h6 41 ♔f2 ♘f5 42 ♘c2 f6**

Understandably Kasparov aims for activity with ...f7-f6 and ...g6-g5, but as we shall later on, White is ready for this advance.

42...♘g7 43 g4 f6 44 ♗d3 g5 45 ♗g6! hxg4 46 h5 (Karpov) gives White a very strong passed pawn on h5. 42...♗d7 has been suggested as Black's most sensible move, but it's always very difficult to 'do nothing'...

**43 ♗d3 g5 44 ♗xf5**

Simplifying – we now have a 'good' knight versus 'bad' bishop situation.

**44...♗xf5 45 ♘e3 ♗b1 46 b4**

White still keeps a slight advantage, but so far Black has defended well, and after, say, 46...♗g6 it's hard to see how White can make any progress. Black's next move, however, is a mistake, although it takes a wonderful reply by Karpov to show why.

**46...gxh4? 47 ♘g2!!**

A truly brilliant move. White temporarily sacrifices a pawn in order to create a square (h4) via which his king can penetrate.

**47...hxg3+**

Or 47...h3 48 ♘f4 and White will eventually pick up both h-pawns, for example 48...♗f5 49 ♘xh5 ♚e7 50 ♘f4, followed by g3-g4.

**48 ♚xg3 ♚e6**

Or 48...♗g6 49 ♘f4 ♗e8 50 ♚h4 and White picks up the h5-pawn.

**49 ♘f4+ ♚f5 50 ♘xh5**

Now White threatens ♘g7-e8-c7, so

Black's king is forced to retreat. Slowly but surely Karpov's king is allowed to penetrate Black's defences.

**50...♚e6 51 ♘f4+ ♚d6 52 ♚g4 ♗c2 53 ♚h5 ♗d1 54 ♚g6**

**54...♚e7**

The beginning of the end. Kasparov tries a desperate pawn sacrifice, but after 54...♗xf3 55 ♚xf6 White eventually wins the d-pawn, for example 55...♗d1 56 ♘g2 ♗g4 57 ♘e3 ♗e2 58 ♘f5+ ♚d7 59 ♚e5 ♗f3 60 ♘e3 ♚c6 61 ♚e6 ♗e2 62 ♘f5 ♗g4 63 ♚e5 ♗f3 (63...♗xf5 64 ♚xf5 is a winning king and pawn ending for White) 64 ♘e7+.

**55 ♘xd5+ ♚e6 56 ♘c7+ ♚d7 57 ♘xa6 ♗xf3 58 ♚xf6 ♚d6 59 ♚f5 ♚d5 60 ♚f4 ♗h1 61 ♚e3 ♚c4 62 ♘c5 ♗c6 63 ♘d3 ♗g2 64 ♘e5+ ♚c3 65 ♘g6 ♚c4 66 ♘e7 ♗b7 67 ♘f5 ♗g2 68 ♘d6+ ♚b3 69 ♘xb5 ♚a4 70 ♘d6 1-0**

# CHAPTER SIX

## Majorities and Minorities

Very often in chess, pawn exchanges lead to an asymmetrical structure, where both sides have pawn majorities (and similarly pawn minorities). The handling of these structures can be the key to either success or failure.

### Exploiting a Mobile Majority

A mobile pawn majority can be a very potent weapon. A player can exploit his extra pawn to either gain space, start an attack, control more squares or create a passed pawn. If one side has a mobile majority, while his opponent's is either restrained or crippled by a weakness, then this is a similar effect to simply being a pawn up.

### M.Gurevich-Hauchard
Belfort 1998

White's advantages in the diagram are the following:

1) He has a lead in development.

2) He has active pieces.

3) Black has problems developing the c8-bishop due to the pressure on the b7-pawn.

How can White make the most of these pluses?

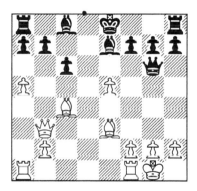

**20 f4!**

The correct plan. With this move White is beginning to utilise his pawn majority. It's quite instructive to see how Gurevich doesn't become distracted by irrelevant features, concentrating purely on how to capitalise on his extra space and material on the kingside.

**20...0-0 21 &d3!**

Taking over an important diagonal, which White needs to control if he wishes to advance with f4-f5.

21 ♖ad1 looks like a natural move, but it's not necessarily helping White's cause, for example 21...♗g4 22 ♖d2 ♖ad8! solves some problems for Black, as both 23 ♖xd8 ♖xd8 24 ♕xb7 ♗h3 25 ♖f2 ♗h4! and 23 ♕xb7? ♖xd2 24 ♗xd2 ♗c5+ 25 ♔h1 ♗h3! are undesirable for White.

**21...♕e6**

21...♗f5 simply loses material after 22 ♗xf5 ♕xf5 23 ♕xb7.

**22 ♕c2!**

Gaining a tempo by hitting the h7-pawn. In any case, on this occasion White's majority is more powerful with the queens on, as it can be used as the beginning of an offensive against the black king. 22 ♕xe6? ♗xe6 23 f5 ♗d5 rather lets Black off the hook.

**22...h6 23 ♔h1 ♔h8**

Black is so cramped that it's difficult to suggest a useful move. Trying to restrain White's majority with 23...g6? is just asking for trouble here, for example 24 f5 gxf5 25 ♗xf5 ♕xe5 26 ♗xh6 ♗d6 27 ♗h7+ ♔h8 28 ♗f4 and Black's king is completely devoid of shelter.

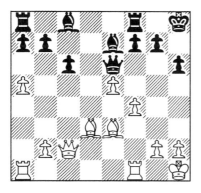

**24 ♖ae1!**

Many less experienced players would automatically grab the open d-file with 24 ♖ad1, or would be afraid of problems involving ...♗b4, but Gurevich's move shows his deep understanding of the position. With the rook on e1, White indirectly supports the e5-pawn in readiness for the surge with f4-f5.

**24...♗b4 25 ♖e2 f5**

Hauchard feels obliged to prevent f4-f5 at any cost, the price being that White now has a powerful protected passed pawn on e5.

25...♗xa5 allows White to carry out his plan with 26 f5! ♕d5 (26...♕xe5 27 ♗c5 wins) 27 ♗c4 (27 f6 also looks strong) 27...♕xe5 28 f6! (28 ♗b6 ♕xe2 29 ♕xe2 ♗xb6 30 ♕e7 also looks good) 28...♗c7 29 ♗g1! ♕g5 30 fxg7+ ♕xg7 (30...♔xg7 loses after 31 ♗d4+ ♔g8 32 ♗xf7+ ♖xf7 33 ♖e8+)

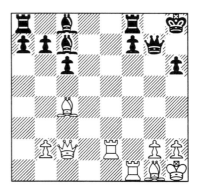

31 ♖xf7! (it's hardly surprising White has some flashy tactic; for the more restrained, 31 ♖e7 looks just as efficient) 31...♖xf7 32 ♖e8+ ♖f8 33 ♖xf8+ ♕xf8 34 ♗d4+ ♕g7 35 ♕g6 and White mates.

**26 ♗c4 ♕e7 27 e6**

Gurevich immediately tries to cash in on his main advantage before Black has any time to consolidate.

**27...♗xa5**

In his notes in *Informator* Gurevich offers 27...♗xe6 as an improvement, for example 28 ♗f2 (28 ♗xe6 ♕xe6 29 ♗c5 ♕xe2 30 ♕xe2 ♗xc5 31 ♕c4 gives White the advantage, but Black has some drawing chances) 28...♖f6 29 ♗h4 and now 29...♕f7? 30 ♖xe6! ♖xe6 31 ♕b3 (Gurevich) is winning for White, but 29...♕c5! is a stronger defence. Then I think White's best line is 30 ♖c1 (30 ♗xf6 ♕xc4 is not so clear) 30...♕xc4 31 ♕xc4 ♗xc4 32 ♖xc4 g5 33 ♖xb4 gxh4 34 ♖xb7 ♖d6 35 ♔g1 and White has good chances to convert his advantage.

**20 ♗d4**

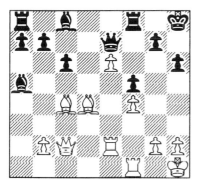

Now Black is completely tied up and developing the queenside will be an accomplishment in itself.

**28...♖d8?**

This leaves the f5-pawn unguarded and White now wins easily. However, 28...b5 29 ♗b3 (with the idea of ♗c5) 29...♗b6 30 ♗xb6 axb6 31 ♕xc6 is grim for Black, while after 28...♗b6 29 ♗c3, how does Black develop?

**29 ♗e5 b5**

Of course 29...♗xe6 loses after 30 ♗xe6 ♕xe6 31 ♗xg7+.

**30 ♗a2 c5 31 ♕xf5 1-0**

With the fall of this pawn, Black's position collapses. There is no good de-

fence to 32 ♗b1.

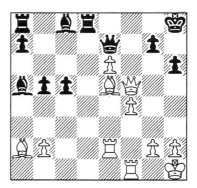

## Queenside Pawn Majorities

In certain queenless middlegames and endgames a mobile queenside majority is viewed more favourably than a kingside pawn majority. More often than not, kings find themselves on the kingside – castling short is far more popular than castling long! Thus the player who possesses the queenside pawn majority does not have to worry about an opposing king stalling his progress or defending the 'pawn minority'.

I should say that the advantage of the queenside pawn majority has in the past been overemphasised by certain writers and players. I've even heard players talk of the advantage of the queenside pawn majority when both kings are on the queenside! Practical experience has taught me that there are often certain features in a position that are more important. Nevertheless, with all other things being equal, the queenside pawn majority is still a useful acquisition.

**Timman-Short**
Riga 1995

Black has an undisputed advantage

here due to two main reasons:

1) The knight has a useful outpost on d3.

2) Black's queenside pawn majority is more threatening than White's kingside pawn majority.

Black's majority is stronger because it's further advanced, well supported and White's king is in the wrong position to contain it – it would prefer to be on the queenside! Black's one 'weakness' is the isolated pawn on e6. I put the word 'weakness' in inverted commas because a pawn is only really weak if it can be attacked. Here White has no beneficial way to do this. Besides, the pawn actually serves a very useful function on e6 (as opposed to a pawn on f6) as it covers the d5-square, which would otherwise be a handy outpost for White.

**19...♔f7**

There is no reason to castle kingside. Black's king is quite safe on f7, where it is well centralised and protects the e6-pawn.

**20 ♗d4 ♘d3 21 ♖ab1**

Perhaps White should consider the immediate 21 b3.

**21...♗e7 22 b3 e5! 23 ♗e3**

Alternatively:

a) 23 bxc4? exd4 24 ♖xd3 bxc4 is winning for Black as 25 ♖xd4 ♗c5 pins the rook to the white king.

b) 23 ♗b6 ♖c6! 24 bxc4 ♖xb6 25 ♖xd3 bxc4 26 ♖dd1 (26 ♖xb6? cxd3 and ...♗c5+ wins for Black) 26...♖d8 with a clear advantage according to Short – the passed c-pawn remains a big threat.

**23...♖hd8 24 bxc4 ♖xc4!**

After this move Black's superiority is becoming more and more obvious. Black's plan is not always necessarily to create a passed pawn on the queenside, but often to simply leave White with a weak 'pawn minority'. Here, as is often in these cases, 'the pawn minority' (that is White's isolated pawn on a2!) is a very susceptible to attack. This fact, added to Black's control of the c-file and a strong knight on d3, adds up to more or less a winning advantage for Black.

On the other hand, in this particular case creating a passed pawn is not so effective. The variation 24...bxc4 25 ♘c3 ♗b4 26 ♘d5 ♗c5 27 ♗xc5 ♖xc5 28 ♘c3 is not so clear – the white knight is a very good blocker of the passed pawn and it's not obvious how Black progresses.

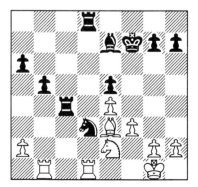

**25 ♔f1 ♖c2?!**

Short prefers 25...♘b4! 26 ♖xd8 ♗xd8 27 ♖b2 ♘c2, after which Black follows up with logical ...a6-a5-a4 and ...b5-b4. White's rook on b2 would then be restricted to a very passive role.

**26 a4!**

A chance to break out of the bind on the queenside.

**26...b4!**

Not the capture 26...bxa4? when 27 ♖b7 in reply, with ideas of ♖xe7+ and ♗g5, gives White undeserved counterplay.

**27 a5?!**

According to Short, White's last chance lies with 27 ♖b3 ♘c5 28 ♖xd8 ♘xb3, although Black still keeps a substantial advantage.

**27...♘b2! 28 ♖xd8 ♗xd8 29 ♗b6 ♗g5**

Now Black is in total control and the passed b-pawn will very soon be a winner.

**30 g3 b3 31 f4 ♘c4! 32 ♖xb3**

Or 32 ♔e1 ♘d2 33 ♖d1 ♗e7 and there is no good answer to ...b3-b2.

**32...♘d2+ 33 ♔e1 ♘xb3 34 fxg5 ♖c4 0-1**

Black's material advantage is sufficient for an easy win.

**Grosar-Rytshagov**
Yerevan Olympiad 1996

In the diagram position you could say that White's advantages lie with the queenside pawn majority and control of the d-file. The second plus point, however, is only imaginary, as Black can contest the file on his very first move.

**20...♖c8?**

As Black in any case decides to exchange rooks later on, this move turns out to be a waste of time. Russian grandmaster Valery Chekhov gives the variation 20...♖d8! (my exclamation mark) 21 ♖xd8+ ♗xd8 22 ♘e4!? ♘xe4 23 ♗xd8 f6 24 f3 ♘d6 25 b3 e5 26 ♔f2 ♔f7 27 ♔e3 ♔e6. In this position Black has a good centralised king and a solid kingside pawn structure – the e5-pawn gives his good central control. White's advantage should not be sufficient to cause Black any real problems.

**21 b3 ♔f8 22 ♔f1 ♔e8 23 ♔e2 ♖d8 24 h3 ♖xd3 25 ♔xd3 ♔d7 26 ♗e3 e5 27 c5!**

An important move. White plans ♔c4 and a general advance of the queenside pawns.

**27...♔e6 28 ♔c4 ♘d7 29 b4 f5 30 f3**

So that the bishop can remain on the g1-a7 diagonal after ...f5-f4.

**30...♗d8 31 a4 h5 32 b5**

White's majority is much quicker and thus more dangerous than Black's.

**32...axb5+ 33 ♘xb5!**

33 axb5, keeping the pawns connected, looks at first sight more logical, but White's choice leaves his king a way through to penetrate the queenside.

**33...g6**

Or 33...♗e7 34 ♘c7+ ♔f7 35 ♔b5. White will continue with c5-c6, leaving him with a very powerful outside passed pawn on the a-file.

**34 ♘d6 b6 35 ♘b7! ♗c7 36 ♔b5 bxc5**

**37 ♔c6!**

The quickest route to victory. White's passed a-pawn will decide matters.

**37...♗b6**

Or 37...♗b8 38 ♘xc5+ ♘xc5 39 ♗xc5 e4 40 fxe4 fxe4 41 a5 ♔f5 42 a6 ♔f4 43 ♔b7 and White wins.

**38 ♗xc5! 1-0**

38...♘xc5 39 ♘xc5+ ♗xc5 40 ♔xc5 gives White a winning king and pawn ending due to the outside passed pawn, for example 40...e4 41 fxe4 fxe4 42 ♔d4 ♔f5 43 ♔e3 ♔e5 44 a5 ♔d5 45 a6 ♔c6 46 ♔xe4 ♔b6 47 ♔f4.

**Lee-Emms**
British League 1999

The diagram position is another example where White has a queenside pawn majority. Here Black can quickly contest the d-file with ...♖fd8. Just as importantly, he can also activate his king reasonably quickly with ...f7-f6, ...♔f7 (and perhaps ...e6-e5 and ...♔e6). This slight difference from the previous example makes Black's position more comfortable. I would actually consider this position to be fairly level and I was reasonably happy to enter it myself, having been reassured of Black's chances from studying two previous games.

**16 ♘c3!**

This is the most natural and the best move. After 16 ♘c3 the game should be completely level – Black can show that the queenside pawn majority isn't the only important factor. As I said before, I was happy to enter this endgame based on two similar ones I had seen, both involving the German grandmaster Christopher Lutz as the black player. On both occasions he created winning chances with Black from a seemingly dead drawn position, and ended up scoring 1½/2. In both games his opponents played the weaker 16 ♘d2? ♘d6! (16...♘xd2?! 17 ♖xd2 ♖fd8 18 ♖ad1 ♗g5 19 ♗e3! ♗xe3 20 fxe3 ♖xd2 21 ♖xd2 with control of the d-file is White's idea) 17 b3 ♖fd8 18 ♘f3 f6! (preparing to gain space with ...e6-e5 and to introduce the king via f7) 19 ♗c5 ♔f7

and now:

a) 20 ♖e1 ♘f5 21 ♗xe7 ♘xe7 22 ♖ed1 ♘c6 (The knights make a very big difference! With these on the board Black's central control offered by his extra e-pawn more than makes up for White's queenside pawn majority. The point is that Black's knight is much more likely to find a good outpost in the cen-

tre of the board.) 23 ♘e1 g5 (Black begins to gain space) 24 ♔f1 h5 25 ♘c2 f5 26 ♔e2 ♔f6 27 ♖xd8 ♖xd8 28 ♖d1 ♖xd1 29 ♔xd1 ♔e5 30 ♔d2 ♘d4 and Black was better in Keitlinghaus-Lutz, German Championship 1997.

b) 20 ♖d2 b6 21 ♗xd6 (after 21 ♗b4 ♘e4 22 ♖xd8 ♖xd8 23 ♗xe7 ♔xe7 Black enjoys control of the d-file – Lutz) 21...♖xd6 22 ♖ad1 ♖ad8 23 ♖xd6 ♗xd6! (Black keeps a pair of rooks on and gives control of the d-file back to White. But with Black's king and bishop covering entry squares on the d-file, the control of this file is less important than usual. Lutz instructively uses his rook to help both a majority attack on the kingside and a minority attack on the queenside!) 24 ♔f1 e5 25 ♔e2 ♔e6 26 ♘e1 h5 27 ♘c2 h4 28 ♘e3 g6 29 ♘d5 f5 30 ♘c3 ♖c8 31 ♘b5 ♗c5 32 ♘c3 ♗d4 33 ♘b5 ♗c5 34 ♘c3 a6 35 ♘d5 b5 36 cxb5 axb5 37 ♘c3 ♖b8 38 ♔f1 b4 39 ♘d5 ♖b7 40 ♘e3 ♗xc3 41 fxe3, Papaioannou-Lutz, Elista Olympiad 1998. White's queenside pawn majority is crippled and he has weaknesses on e3 and a2. Lutz went on to convert these advantages into an impressive win.

**16...♘xc3**

16...♘d6? no longer works. After 17 ♗c5 ♖fd8 18 ♘e4 ♘xe4 19 ♗xe7 ♖xd1+ 20 ♖xd1 White, who plans ♖d7, is in control.

**17 ♗xc3 ♖fd8**

Of course Black must contest the d-file. In Lutz's words, 'both players centralise their kings, exchange all the rooks and a draw can be signed.'

**18 b3 f6**

The kingside pawns must expand and the black king enters the game.

**19 ♔f1 ♔f7 20 ♔e2 e5**

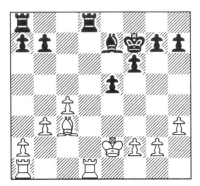

**21 ♗d2!?**

A sign that my opponent was trying to liven up the game, which I have to admit until now hadn't been the most fascinating of encounters. For this reason I must give him some credit, although objectively speaking perhaps White should whip off the remaining rooks with 21 ♖xd8 ♖xd8 22 ♖d1 ♖xd1 23 ♔xd1 ♔e6 24 ♔e2 f5 25 f3 and offer a draw!

I guess I was quite happy to see this move, as at least I now felt that there would be possible chances to gain an advantage.

**21...♔e6 22 ♗e3 a6 23 ♗b6**

This is White's idea.

**23...♖xd1 24 ♖xd1**

So White now controls the open d-file, but with Black's king so well placed on e6, White can never really gain much advantage from this. White's plan is now c4-c5, followed by ♔d3-c4 and the advance of the queenside pawns. This all looks logical, but there is a drawback to this idea, as we shall see.

**24...h5!**

Black must start to push his majority. It may seem a bit flippant to say so, but in a race of pawn majorities, you want your pawns as far up the board as possible!

**25 c5**

Part of White's plan, but all the same very committal, as now the bishop on b6 has no influence on the events going on behind him. It's still not too late for White to hunker down for the draw with 25 f3.

**25...f5 26 ♔d3 g5 27 ♔c4 g4**

By this stage it's becoming apparent that Black's majority attack is more dangerous than White's. The next idea is to swap on h3 then occupy the g-file so my opponent played...

**28 hxg4?**

But this turn out to be a decisive mistake. In my opinion, White should leave the kingside and continue with the general advance after 28 b4!, for example 28...gxh3 29 gxh3 ♖g8 30 a4 ♖g2 31 ♖d2 and now:

a) 31...♖h2 32 b5 axb5+ 33 axb5 ♖xh3 34 c6 and White's c-pawn is quite dangerous. One line is 34...bxc6 35 bxc6 ♖h1 36 c7 ♖c1+ 37 ♔b5 ♗d6 38 ♖d1! ♖c2 39 ♖d2! and Black has nothing better than to repeat moves.

b) 31...e4 32 b5 axb5+ 33 axb5 e3 34 ♖e2 f4 35 c6 bxc6 36 bxc6 seems to be okay for White, for example 36...♗h4? 37 c7 ♔d7 38 ♖a2 ♖xf2 39 ♖a8 ♖c2+ 40 ♔d3 ♖xc7 41 ♗xc7 ♔xc7 42 ♖a5 and Black certainly isn't winning here!

**28...fxg4!**

This move gives Black a potential outside passed pawn on the h-file, while the f2-pawn will also be vulnerable (a consequence of White's 25th move).

**29 g3**

29 ♖h1 is simply answered by 29...h4.

**29...♖f8 30 ♖d2 h4**

This pawn has to be captured.

**31 gxh4 ♖f4+ 32 ♔c3 ♗xh4**

Now White's only chance is to keep hold of f2 by giving up a pawn with c5-c6.

**33 ♖d6+? ♔f5 34 ♖d7 ♗xf2 35 ♖xb7 g3**

Black's pawn is quicker.

**36 c6 ♗xb6 37 ♖xb6 ♖f1 38 ♔d2 g2 39 c7**

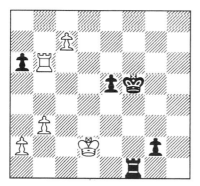

**39...♖c1! 0-1**

40 ♔xc1 g1♕+ 41 ♔b2 ♕c5 42 ♖b7 e4 and Black wins.

### The Minority Attack

A minority attack is just how it sounds; it's an attack by a minority (of pawns) against a majority, the aim of which it to inflict one or more pawn weaknesses on the majority. A minority attack works better in certain formations; Black's advance of his queenside pawns in an Open Sicilian is one example, but the most common formation for a minority attack arises from the Exchange Variation of the Queen's Gambit Declined.

**Ruban-Panchenko**
Elista 1994
*Queen's Gambit Declined*

1 d4 ♘f6 2 c4 e6 3 ♘f3 d5 4 ♘c3 c6 5 ♗g5 ♘bd7 6 cxd5 exd5 7 e3 ♗e7 8 ♗d3 0-0 9 ♕c2 ♖e8 10 0-0 ♘f8

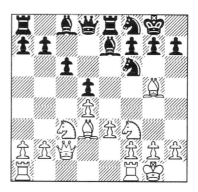

So far we've reached a typical position from the Exchange Variation of the Queen's Gambit Declined (those wishing for an intimate knowledge of the QGD could do worse than acquiring Matthew Sadler's brilliant *Queen's Gambit Declined*, which is also published by Everyman).

In this particular position White's strongest and most straightforward idea is the minority attack involving the advance b4-b5. This will force Black to accept some sort of pawn weakness. If

Black captures on b5, or if he allows White to capture with bxc6 and he recaptures with a piece, he will be left with an isolated d-pawn. If he allows bxc6 and recaptures with ...bxc6 then he will be left with a backward c-pawn. The final possibility for Black is to advance with ...c6-c5, but after an exchange on c5 Black will still be left with an isolated pawn.

**11 h3**

Of course White could also begin with the direct 11 ♖ab1 (see the next game) or 11 a3, both of which prepare for b2-b4. There is, however, much to be said for this prophylactic measure on the kingside, which rules out black ideas of ...♗g4 and answering ♘e5 with ...♘g4. One further point is that White's dark-squared bishop can sometimes find a safe haven in the h2-square.

**11...g6**

A typical idea for Black in this line. With this move Black prepares the manoeuvre ...♘e6-g7, followed by ...♗f5. This exchanges the c8-bishop, Black's problem piece, which has been further restricted by White's h2-h3.

Sensible alternatives for Black include 11...♘g6, 11...♘e4 and 11...♗e6.

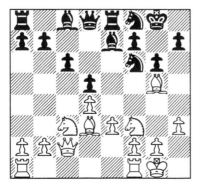

**12 ♖ab1**

Finally White prepares for the thematic b2-b4-b5.

**12...♘e6**

12...a5 forces White to play with an extra preparatory move 13 a3, but following 13...♘e6 14 ♗h6 play could well transpose into main text with 14...♘g7 15 b4 axb4 16 axb4 ♗f5.

**13 ♗h6**

13 ♗h4 is also possible, after which Black still follows up with ...♘g7 and ...♗f5.

**13...♘g7 14 b4 a6 15 a4**

Ensuring that White will be able to get in b4-b5. A slightly more refined plan is to aim to locate the knight on c5 first with 15 ♘a4, for example 15...♗f5 16 ♗xg7 ♗xd3 17 ♕xd3 ♔xg7 18 ♘c5 ♖b8 and only now 19 a4.

**15...♗f5**

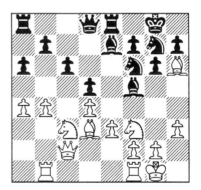

**16 ♗xg7**

White chops some wood before playing b4-b5. This isn't the only way, however. White has other choices, for example:

a) 16 ♘e5 ♖c8! (this makes the advance b4-b5 more problematic for White) 17 ♗xg7 ♗xd3 18 ♘xd3 ♔xg7 19 ♖b3 ♗d6! (preventing ♘e5) 20 b5?

(Ivanchuk gives 20 ♕b2 ♔g8 21 b5 axb5 22 axb5 c5 with an equal position; after an exchange on c5 Black will have an IQP but White's major pieces look a bit strange on the blocked b-file) 20...cxb5! 21 axb5 a5 22 ♕b2 b6!

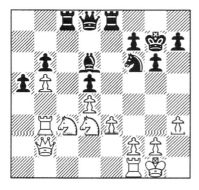

and Black has dealt with the minority attack in a very efficient way. The d-pawn is isolated but White finds it difficult to get at. Meanwhile, Black has control of the open c-file, White's major pieces are bunched on the closed b-file and Black has a useful protected passed pawn on a5. The game Gelfand-Ivanchuk, Linares 1993 continued 23 ♘a4 ♖c4 24 ♖a1 ♘e4 25 f3 ♘g3 26 ♘e5 ♗xe5 27 dxe5 ♕c7 28 ♔h2 ♘f5 29 f4 ♖c2 30 ♖c3 ♖xc3 31 ♕xc3 ♕xc3 32 ♘xc3 ♘xe3 and Black went on to win.

b) 16 b5 (there doesn't seem to be much wrong with this direct approach) 16...axb5 (Now 16...cxb5?! 17 axb5 a5 is not so effective: 18 ♗xf5 ♘xf5 19 ♗g5! and suddenly the d5-pawn is extremely vulnerable to attack) 17 axb5 ♖a3 18 ♖a1 ♗xd3 19 ♕xd3 ♕a5 20 ♖xa3 ♕xa3 21 ♘e5 ♘e4 22 ♘xe4 ♕xd3 23 ♘f6+! ♗xf6 24 ♘xd3 and White keeps an edge – Ivanchuk.

**16...♗xd3  17 ♕xd3  ♔xg7  18 b5**

**axb5**

Hjartarson suggests the ides of 18...cxb5!? 19 axb5 a5, as in the Gelfand-Ivanchuk game above. There is certainly something to be said about this approach, although in this particular example White's pieces are better placed and he can consider putting a fly in the ointment with 20 b6, not allowing Black to consolidate with ...b7-b6.

**19 axb5 ♖a3**

If you think you've seen this position before, you may be right! The moves up until 19...♖a3 had all been played before at grandmaster level. Ruban's next move is actually a useful novelty, improving upon 20 ♕c2? ♕a5! 21 ♖b3 ♖c8!, as in van Wely-Hjartarson, Akureyri 1994.

**20 bxc6! bxc6**

Or 20...♕a5 21 ♖fc1 and now:

a) 21...♘e4? fails to 22 ♕b5! ♘xc3 23 ♕xa5 ♖xa5 24 ♖xc3.

b) 21...♗b4? runs into 22 cxb7 ♖b8 23 ♘e5 and White is winning   Ruban, for example 23...♖xc3 24 ♖xc3 ♗xc3 25 ♘c6, or 23...♗xc324 ♘c6 ♗d2 25 ♕f1 ♕c7 26 ♘xb8 ♗xc1 27 ♘a6.

**21 ♕c2 ♕a5 22 ♖fc1**

The minority attack is finally completed, rewarding White with a backward c-pawn as an object of attack. On the other hand, Black is quite active and it's unlikely that, with best play, this one weakness will win the game for White.

**22...♗b4?!**

22...c5 23 ♖b5 ♕a6 24 ♕b2! (Ruban) is awkward for Black, but Sadler rightly prefers 22...♗d6 ('it is clear that in general the black bishop belongs on the active d6-square'). Sadler follows this up with the interesting variation 23 ♖b7 ♖b8 24 ♖xb8 ♗xb8 25 ♘b1?! (this is too risky) 25...♖a2 26 ♕xc6 ♘e4 27 ♘c3? ♘xc3 28 ♖xc3 ♕b6! (exploiting the weak back rank and justifying 22...♗d6) 29 ♘e5 ♖a1+ 30 ♔h2 ♕xc6 31 ♖xc6 f6 32 ♖b6 ♗c7 33 ♖c6 ♖a7! and Black wins material.

**23 ♖b3**

Ruban prefers retreating with 23 ♘e2!, for example 23...♖a2 24 ♖b2 ♖xb2 25 ♕xb2 ♗a3 26 ♕a2! ♖b8 27 ♖a1 ♖a8 28 ♕c2 and the c-pawn weakness is becoming more and more obvious.

**23...♖c8 24 ♖xa3 ♕xa3 25 ♘b1 ♕a6 26 ♘e5 ♗d6 27 ♘d3 ♘d7 28 ♘c3 ♘f6 29 ♘a4 h5?! 30 ♘ac5 ♗xc5 31 ♘xc5 ♕a7 32 ♕d1!**

Compared to just a few moves ago, White now has a firm grip on the posi-

tion and Black is tied down to the defensive task of protecting his weak c6-pawn. In the game this proved too difficult for Panchenko.

**32...♕e7 33 ♕a4! ♘e4 34 ♕a6! ♘d6 35 ♘d3 ♕b7 36 ♕xb7 ♘xb7 37 ♘b4 c5 38 dxc5 ♖xc5 39 ♖xc5 ♘xc5 40 ♘xd5 h4? 41 f4!.**

This seals the win. The h4-pawn is vulnerable.

**41...♘e4 42 ♔f1 f5 43 ♔e2 g5 44 fxg5 ♔g6 45 ♘f4+ ♔xg5 46 ♘e6+ ♔f6 47 ♘d4! ♘c3+ 48 ♔d3 ♘d5 49 ♘f3 f4 50 e4 ♘b4+ 51 ♔c3 ♘c6 52 ♔c4 ♔e6 53 ♘d4+ ♔e5 54 ♘xc6+ ♔xe4 55 ♘d4 ♔e3 56 ♘f3! ♔f2 57 ♘xh4 ♔g3 58 ♔d4 ♔xh4**

**59 ♔e4! 1-0**

59...♔g3 60 h4! wins for White.

The following example is another smooth performance by Karpov, who successfully implements the minority attack.

**Karpov-Ljubojevic**
Linares 1989
*Queen's Gambit Declined*

**1 d4 ♘f6 2 c4 e6 3 ♘c3 d5 4 cxd5**

**exd5 5 ♗g5 c6 6 e3 ♘bd7 7 ♗d3 ♗e7 8 ♕c2 0-0 9 ♘f3 ♖e8 10 0-0 ♘f8 11 ♖ab1**

This time White dispenses with h2-h3 and aims directly for b2-b4-b5.

**11...♘e4**

A typical simplifying procedure, although Black has many other moves, including 11...♘g6, 11....♗d6 and 11...a5 12 a3 ♗d6!?.

**12 ♗xe7 ♕xe7 13 b4**

Here it comes!

**13...a6 14 a4 ♗f5**

Supporting the knight on e4. After 14...♘g6 15 b5 axb5 16 axb5 ♗g4 17 ♗xe4! dxe4 18 ♘d2 ♗f5 19 bxc6 bxc6 20 ♘e2 ♘h4 21 ♘g3 ♗g6 22 ♕xc6 White has dealt with any kingside threats and has nabbed the weak c6-pawn, Averbakh-Konstantinopolsky, Moscow 1966.

**15 ♘e5**

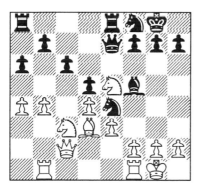

**15...♖ad8**

Or 15...f6 16 ♗xe4 ♗xe4 17 ♘xe4 fxe5 (17...dxe4 18 ♘c4 leaves Black with a potentially vulnerable e4-pawn, while White will still continue the attack on the queenside with b4-b5) 18 ♘g3 (18 ♘c5!?) 18...exd4 19 ♘f5 with an edge for White – Karpov. This looks like a good

assessment, for example 19...♕f6 20 ♘xd4 ♘e6 21 ♘xe6 ♖xe6 22 b5 axb5 23 axb5 and Black will wind up with a pawn weakness of some sort.

**16 ♖fc1**

Defending c5, which is important in some lines. The immediate 16 ♘xe4 is not so effective after 16...♗xe4 17 ♗xe4 dxe4 18 b5 axb5 19 axb5 c5! – Karpov.

**16...♘g6 17 ♗xe4 ♗xe4 18 ♘xe4 dxe4?!**

Karpov gives the line 18...♘xe5!? 19 ♘d2 ♘g6 20 b5 axb5 21 axb5 ♖d6 with only a slight advantage to White. The rook on d6 is well placed – it defends the vulnerable c6-pawn and can also swing over to the kingside and be used as an attacking weapon against the white king.

**19 ♘xg6 hxg6**

**20 b5!**

Black's pawn on e4 could well become insecure, especially in a rook ending, while White's minority attack will induce another pawn weakness in the black camp. With two such worries, Black will find it very difficult to defend.

**20...cxb5 21 axb5 ♖d6**

21...a5? 22 b6! leaves both the a5- and b7-pawns precariously placed.

**22 bxa6 bxa6 23 ♕a4 ♕d7?!**

Exchanging queens merely eases White's overall task. Karpov prefers grim defence with 23...罝a8.

**24 豐xd7 罝xd7 25 罝c5! 罝a7 26 罝a5**

The pawn weaknesses on a6 and e4 are particularly worrisome for Black in this double rook ending.

**26...堂f8 27 罝b6 罝ea8 28 h4!**

A nice move. Karpov prepares the simple 堂h2-g3-f4.

**28...堂e7 29 堂h2 堂d7**

Black's king must rush to the queenside in order to free one of his rooks.

**30 堂g3 堂c7 31 罝b2 罝b7 32 罝c5+ 堂b8 33 罝a2 罝e7 34 堂f4 堂b7 35 罝b2+ 堂a7 36 罝c6!**

Preparing 罝bb6!.

**36...罝h8 37 罝a2! a5**

37...罝xh4+ loses after 38 堂g3 罝h5 39 罝cxa6+ 堂b8 40 罝a8+ 堂c7 41 罝2a7+ 堂d6 42 罝d8+ 堂c6 43 罝xe7.

**38 罝xa5+ 堂b7 39 罝ca6 罝xh4+ 40 堂g3 罝h5**

**41 罝a7+ 堂c6 42 罝5a6+ 堂b5 43 罝xe7 罝g5+ 44 堂h2 堂xa6 45 罝xf7 1-0**

The single rook ending is hopeless.

We've already seen certain methods which Black can adopt against the minority attack. The following example shows one of the most popular ways of drawing the sting from White's plan.

**Bick-Korneev**
Linares 2000

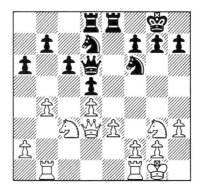

Here White would obviously like to implement a minority attack with a2-a4 and b4-b5, but on this occasion Black has a very effective antidote...

**15...b5!**

This certainly prevents White's plan. The lunge ...b7-b5 works in certain situations, this being one of them. In particular it helps that Black has a knight on d7, which is ready to manoeuvre via b6 to the c4-outpost, where it will conveniently shield Black's backward c-pawn. Another plus point for Black is that White is in no position to play a favourable ♘e5, which would again put the c6-pawn under pressure.

**16 a4 ♘b6!**

Played just in time before White has a chance to prevent the manoeuvre with a4-a5.

**17 a5 ♘c4**

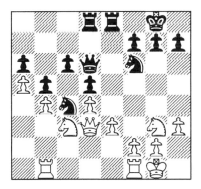

In the game White now blundered with 18 ♖fd1? ♘xe3! and Black won quickly. 18 ♖fe1, with the idea of ♘f1-d2, is stronger although if anything I already prefer Black.

Minority attacks usually occur on the queenside, but there are exceptions. In the following endgame I was able to im-

plement an attack on the other wing.

**Emms-Etchegaray**
Cappelle la Grande 1994

A double rook ending has arisen. How should White proceed?

**26 g4!**

White aims to break up the solid black pawn structure on the kingside with f4-f5. This is another version of a minority attack and regardless of how Black reacts, he will be left with at least one weakness on the kingside.

**26...hxg4 27 hxg4 a5**

One further point I should make is that White's queenside structure is doing a good job of slowing down any minority attack that Black may be aiming for on the other wing. The 'normal' 26...b5? is easily answered by 27 b4! and Black has only succeeded in creating further weaknesses for himself.

**28 f5!**

The logical breakthrough.

**28...gxf5 29 gxf5 ♖g8+ 30 ♔f2 ♖g5 31 ♔f3!**

It's time to use the power of the king. 31 fxe6 ♖xe5 32 dxe5 fxe6 is not so clear, as White's own e5-pawn could become vulnerable.

**31...♔g7**

31...♖xf5+ 32 ♖xf5 exf5 temporarily leaves Black a pawn up, but his structure is awful. Nevertheless, this may be his best chance to complicate matters. Both 33 ♖e1 ♔g6 34 ♖e7 b5 35 ♖d7 ♔g5 36 ♖xd5 ♖h8 37 ♖xb5 ♖h3+ 38 ♔g2 ♖d3 and 33 ♔f4 ♔g6 34 ♖g1+ ♔f6 35 ♖g5 ♔e6 36 ♖xf5 a4 are not totally winning for White.

**32 ♔f4 ♔f6 33 ♖h1 exf5**

33...♖xf5+ 34 ♖xf5+ exf5 35 ♖h6+ ♔e7 36 ♖b6 is horrible for Black.

**34 ♖h6+ ♖g6 35 ♖xf5+ ♔e6 36 ♖hh5**

As in the Karpov game, we see that pawn weaknesses are much more pronounced in double rook endings than in single rook endings.

**36...f6 37 ♖xd5 ♖ag8 38 ♖b5 ♖g4+ 39 ♔f3 ♖g3+ 40 ♔e2 ♖g2+ 41 ♔d3 ♖8g3+ 42 ♔c4 ♖xb2 43 ♖xb7**

White has an extra pawn and the passed d-pawn will be decisive.

**43...♖c2 44 d5+ ♔d6 45 ♖b6+ ♔d7 46 ♖h7+ ♔c8 47 ♔c5! ♖cxc3+ 48 ♔d6 ♖g8 49 ♖c6+**

The simplest, transposing into a winning single rook ending.

**49...♖xc6+ 50 ♔xc6 ♖f8 51 d6 f5 52 ♖a7 ♔b8 53 ♖b7+ ♔a8 54 d7 1-0**

# CHAPTER SEVEN

## Other Positional Features

In this chapter we look at positional ideas which didn't fit into the previous chapters. These include the concept of space and capacity, colour complexes, prophylaxis and positional sacrifices.

### Space and Capacity

A common annotation used in many chess books is 'White has a space advantage' or 'Black is solid but rather cramped'. How important is a space advantage? Well, most players would fully agree that an abundance of space can certainly be a great advantage, but how many realise that in certain situations a space advantage can actually be a disadvantage?

In *Simple Chess* Michael Stean talked of 'space' and 'capacity' in a way that was quite enlightening to me. His words were, 'Any given pawn structure has a certain capacity for accommodating pieces efficiently. Exceed this capacity and the pieces get in each other's way, and so reduce their mutual activity. The problem of overpopulation is easy to sense when playing a position – it 'feels'

cramped.' Stean goes on to mention that a player can in fact have too much space if he doesn't have the enough piece to patrol all the areas. 'A vast empire requires an army of equal proportions to defend it.'

I would like to talk about space and capacity in relation to one of my favourite openings – the Modern Benoni. Consider the Classical Variation

**1 d4 ♘f6 2 c4 c5 3 d5 e6 4 ♘c3 exd5 5 cxd5 d6 6 e4 g6 7 ♘f3 ♗g7 8 ♗e2 0-0 9 0-0 a6 10 a4**

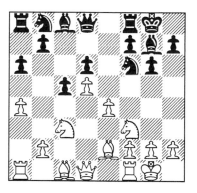

In the eyes of most Benoni experts, Black's structure has the capacity for

three minor pieces, but not four. Thus Black's most popular move in this position is 10...♗g4. Black is quite prepared to give up the bishop pair, even without provocation, if it means that he will be left with the correct number of pieces for his structural capacity. After 11 ♗f4 ♗xf3 12 ♗xf3 ♕e7 13 ♖e1 ♘bd7

we see that Black's position has a certain harmony to it. All the pieces are developed and the rooks are connected. Statistics back up Black's concept – Black's score from the position after 10...♗g4 is a highly respectable 52% in *Mega Database 2001*.

It's certainly true that Black has other plans at his disposal which do not include the exchange of this bishop (for example 9...♖e8 10 ♘d2 ♘bd7 11 a4 ♘e5, although this only scores 43%), but in many of these lines Black suffers from a lack of breathing space.

Perhaps it was Black's excellent score with 10...♗g4 which led to white players searching for new positional ways to combat the Modern Benoni. At the end of the 1980s a new variation began to gain in popularity and these days, this so-called 'Modern Classical' is far more popular than the old 'Classical'.

One move-order for the Modern Classical is as follows:
**1 d4 ♘f6 2 c4 c5 3 d5 e6 4 ♘c3 exd5 5 cxd5 d6 6 ♘f3 g6 7 e4 ♗g7**
and now White plays
**8 h3! 0-0 9 ♗d3**

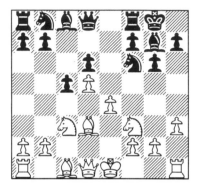

The point of White's move order is simply to eliminate Black's possibility of playing the 'freeing' ...♗g4. Black is stuck with four minor pieces and this exceeds his capacity. Quiet lines from the diagram have produced excellent results for White over the past decade.

Black can try to exploit the non-developing nature of h2-h3 with the very sharp sacrifice 9...b5, which has accrued a vast body of theory, but White holds a theoretical edge in these lines and the forcing nature of the variations is not to everyone's taste.

The story doesn't quite end here though. After White began to score heavily with the Modern Classical, Modern Benoni experts such as the Israeli grandmaster Lev Psakhis put their thinking caps on and came up with a more refined move order:
**1 d4 ♘f6 2 c4 c5 3 d5 e6 4 ♘c3 exd5 5 cxd5 d6 6 ♘f3 g6 7 e4**
and now:

**7...a6! 8 a4 ♗g4!**

and Black has managed to get in his bishop move after all, albeit a little earlier than usual. However, after the natural continuation 9 ♗e2 ♗xf3 10 ♗xf3 ♗g7 11 0-0 0-0 12 ♗f4 ♕e7 13 ♖e1 ♘bd7, Black is reaching his desired position once again!

This seemed to be okay and Black players breathed more easily for a while, but only until White came up with a further refinement:

**1 d4 ♘f6 2 c4 c5 3 d5 e6 4 ♘c3 exd5 5 cxd5 d6 6 ♘f3 g6**

and now

**7 h3!**

Brilliant! White simply prevents ...♗g4 a move earlier. Now 7...♗g7 can be answered by 8 e4 and 7...a6 can be answered by 8 a4, and once again Black is stuck with the four minor pieces. There is, however, one concession that White has to make in this move order. After 7...a6 8 a4 Black can play the move 8...♕e7, after which White is prevented from playing e2-e4 for the moment. However, there are plenty of other ways for White to complete his development and this hasn't stopped many white players turning to the ultra-modern 7 h3!.

## Exploiting Extra Space

You can judge from above that the major rule of thumb when trying to exploit extra space is to avoid exchanges, which would allow the opposition's piece count to be in line with his structural capacity. Of course this is a very general rule and there are many exceptions, for example it may well be worthwhile exchanging a bad bishop for a good one if the opportunity arises.

It's often necessary to be very patient when trying to exploit a space advantage. Your opponent may be lacking in space, but it's likely that his position is still very solid. Storming the barricades may not be the most effective way forward. A calmer approach often pays better dividends. Often the cramped player cannot resist opening up to gain more space, but this can often leave behind structural weakness which can then be exploited.

The following example of exchange avoidance had a very profound effect on me.

### Karpov-Unzicker
Nice Olympiad 1974

The central pawn structure of e4/d5 vs. e5/d6 dictates that White has more space in this position. At the moment Black's number of pieces exceeds his space capacity, so it's natural that he would like to exchange. The likelihood of exchanges seems quite high, given the open a-file, but Karpov finds a visually stunning and very effective way of preventing exchanges.

**24 ♗a7!!**

One exclamation mark for the objective value of this move and one for its originality. In fact I can only find one similar manoeuvre by White before this game, a little known encounter where the Yugoslav grandmaster Aleksandar Matanovic had the white pieces. I wonder if Karpov was aware of this game?

To the merits of the actual move. Firstly, White prevents a mass exchange of major pieces down the a-file. Furthermore, White is now able build up at leisure along the a-file. When the bishop does finally decide to move, White will have undisputed control of that file. Notice that White can only get away with this masterstroke because of Black's problem with piece co-ordination (a by product of a lack of space problem). We've come back to that terrible knight on b7, which prevents an immediate attack on the bishop with ...♕c7.

**24...♘e8**

After 24...♕c7!? 25 ♖a6 ♘d8 26 ♕a2, White will follow up with ♗c2 and ♖a1.

**25 ♗c2 ♘c7 26 ♖ea1 ♕e7 27 ♗b1 ♗e8 28 ♘e2 ♘d8 29 ♘h2**

Karpov plans the pawn break f2-f4.

**29...♗g7 30 f4 f6**

Capturing on f4 opens the long diagonal for the bishop, but on the other hand it presents White with a very useful outpost on d4.

**31 f5 g5 32 ♗c2!**

This bishop is going places!

**32...♗f7 33 ♘g3 ♘b7 34 ♗d1 h6**

**35 ♗h5!**

Finally White permits an exchange, but this is very favourable one for Karpov. White exchanges his 'bad bishop' for Black's 'good bishop'. Furthermore, this leaves Black struggling on the light squares around his own king.

**35...♕e8 36 ♕d1 ♘d8 37 ♖a3 ♔f8**

Black has run out of ideas and can only sit and wait.

**38 ♖1a2 ♔g8 39 ♘g4! ♔f8**

39...♗xh5 40 ♘xh5 ♕xh5 loses to 41 ♘xf6+.

**40 ♘e3 ♔g8 41 ♗xf7+ ♘xf7 42 ♕h5 ♘d8 43 ♕g6 ♔h8 44 ♘h5 1-0**

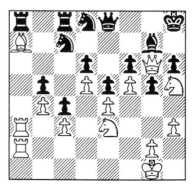

So that bishop never did move from a7. A typical and wonderful display from Karpov.

I never thought I would be able to benefit in such a direct way from remembering this game but, many years later, an opportunity arose.

**Emms-Thipsay**
British Championship, Scarborough 1999

Twenty-five years later and do you spot the similarities? On this occasion Black has managed to exchange one minor piece, but this is not enough to solve his space problems.

**22 ♗a7!**

Only one exclamation mark this time, as by now quite a few players had copied Karpov's idea. I was nevertheless very happy to have been able to implement it in one of my own games.

22 ♕b1 ♘d8 23 ♕b2 ♕b7 would get White nowhere and would simply lead to a period of bloodletting along the open a-file.

**22...♖c8 23 ♖a3?!**

23 ♖a6! would have been very effective here, for example 23...♘d8 (23...♘a5 fails to 24 ♗b6) 24 ♕a1 ♕b7 25 ♕a2

♖c7 26 ♖a1 and White is in total control. **23...♘a5! 24 ♗e3 ♘b3 25 ♖xa8 ♖xa8 26 ♗xb3 cxb3 27 ♕xb3 f5**

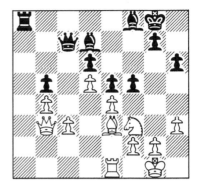

and my opponent had some compensation for the pawn, although objectively I still prefer White and I did manage to win the game in the end.

### Dark Squares and Light Squares

You often come across certain phrases in chess literature such as 'White has good dark square control', or 'Black is weak on the light squares' (there are a number of occasions just in this book). What is meant by this? Put simply, there are occasions where one player controls a large number of squares, usually grouped together, and all of the same colour. This can come about due to a variety of reasons, such as one player possessing a bishop of a certain colour, while his opponent's has already been traded. Another usual prerequisite is for a number of pawns (especially central ones) to all be on a certain colour of square. Often the player in possession of these pawns suffers from lack of control on the opposite colour. Let's once again try and clarify matters by looking at a specific example.

The diagram position shows a typical pawn structure reached when Black plays the Stonewall Variation of the Dutch Defence. By putting his central pawns on c6, d5, e6 and f5, Black has claimed quite a lot of space and has a grip on the e4-square. However, there is a certain price to pay for this. By putting all of his pawns on light squares, the pawns themselves naturally only protect squares of the same colour. This has left Black with the burden of controlling dark squares in the centre by pieces only, whereas White can use pieces *and* pawns (for example the d4-pawn and, to a lesser degree, the g3-pawn).

Black relies heavily on his dark-squared bishop to compensate for his pawn, whereas White's dark-squared bishop doesn't have the same burden. If White were to play &xb2, then he would be leading the control of the e5-square by the score 2-1. However, it makes even greater positional sense for White to seek the exchange of the dark-squared bishops, either by &c1-a3 or &c1-f4. With an exchange of the bishops, White would lead the control over the e5-square by the score 1-0 which, percentage-wise, is better than 2-1. So, on this

occasion, the exchange of the dark-squared bishops increases White's control over the dark squares or, put another way, emphasises Black's weakness on the dark squares.

Control of a colour complex is an especially important concept of modern chess, with many opening and middlegame battles being won and lost in this manner. Here are a couple of examples.

**Kovalenko-Yeremenko**
Kharkov 2000

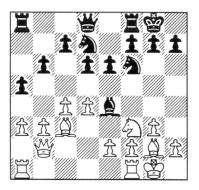

From this tranquil looking position Black puts into effect a plan of light-square domination.

**13...a4!**

Playing on the very slight weakness that White's earlier advance a2-a3 has left. As a consequence, White is unable to keep supporting the c4-pawn.

**14 ♘d2**

Following 14 b4 Black can continue the theme with 14...b5! 15 cxb5 ♕b8 . Black picks up the pawn on b5 and secures the d5-square as a very effective outpost for a knight.

**14...&xg2 15 ♔xg2 ♕b8**

I must admit that I would also have been very tempted by the direct

15...axb3, leaving White with an isolated a-pawn. On second thoughts, however, White would have a very good chance of liquidating the weakness with a4-a5.

Yeremenko's move continues the policy of light-square domination.

**16 b4 b5!**

Excellent play. The d5-square is falling into Black's hands.

**17 c5 ♕b7+ 18 ♔g1**

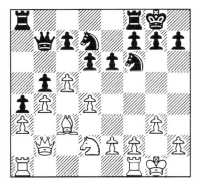

**18...♘h5!?**

Preparing ...f7-f5. Rather than waiting for this to happen, White fights back in the centre.

**19 e4 f5**

Not giving White any time to consolidate.

**20 ♖ae1 ♘hf6 21 ♕c2 f4!?**

There's nothing wrong with this move – in fact it works out well for Black – but a more direct way to continue the light-square policy is with 21...fxe4 22 ♘xe4 ♖ae8.

**22 ♗b2 ♕c6 23 gxf4 d5!**

Continuing the theme. Notice that Black has consigned White with a 'bad bishop' which, on this occasion, really is bad.

**24 f5**

24 e5 ♘h5 picks up the pawn on f4

and leaves Black with good attacking chances down the half-open f-file.

**24...exf5 25 exf5 ♖ae8**

Black is a pawn down, but the f5-pawn is weak and White's bishop on b2 is well out of the game.

**26 ♘f3 ♘e4 27 ♘e5 ♘xe5 28 dxe5 ♖xf5**

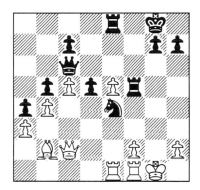

**29 f3?**

This allows a neat combination. 29 f4 is much stronger, although I would still prefer Black's position.

**29...♕g6+! 30 ♔h1 ♘g3+!**

This wins material.

**31 hxg3 ♖h5+ 32 ♕h2 ♖xh2+ 33 ♔xh2 ♕c2+ 0-1**

In the next example Black is quite willing to part with material early on in the game, just so he can get his own way with a colour complex.

**Tregubov-Aseev**
Russian Championship, Samara 2000
*Queen's Indian Defence*

**1 d4 ♘f6 2 c4 e6 3 ♘f3 b6 4 g3 ♗a6 5 ♘bd2 c5 6 ♗g2**

A more aggressive possibility for White is 6 e4.

**6...♘c6 7 ♘e5!?**

This move is very ambitious, perhaps a touch too ambitious.

**7...♘xd4!**

Most grandmasters wouldn't need to think too long before playing a move like this. Black is prepared to give up an exchange for a pawn and plenty of light square control.

A safer way to play would be with 7...♗b7, for example 8 ♘xc6 ♗xc6 9 ♗xc6 dxc6 10 ♕a4 ♕d7 11 dxc5 ♗xc5 12 0-0 0-0 13 ♘f3 ♕b7 with a roughly level position, Solmundarson-Magnusson, Reykjavik 1972.

**8 e3**

This is a refinement on previous theory. White can also grab the exchange immediately with 8 ♗xa8 ♕xa8. Vladimirov-Dautov, Frunze 1988 now continued 9 0-0 ♗e7 10 b3 d6 11 ♘ef3 ♘xf3+ 12 ♘xf3 ♕c6 13 ♗b2 ♗b7 14 h3 0-0 15 ♕c2 ♘e4 16 ♔h2 f5 and it's quite clear that Black has serious compensation for the small material disadvantage.

My overall impression of this line is that it looks more fun to play Black than White, although objectively chances are roughly balanced.

**8...♘f5**

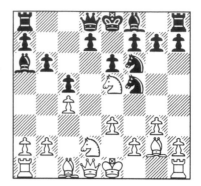

**9 ♕a4**

Once again White delays capturing the rook. It's almost as if he knows what problems he'll have on the light squares so he just doesn't want to grab on a8. However, after already throwing a pawn into the pot, White is fully committed to capturing.

The line 9 ♗xa8 ♕xa8 10 0-0 (this looks like a severe case of 'castling into it') 10...♗d6 11 ♘ef3 h5 (11...♕c6!? intending ...♗b7 – Gershon – should also be considered) 12 ♖e1 ♘e4 13 ♘xe4 ♕xe4 14 ♘d2 ♕c6 15 b3 h4 was also promising for Black in the game Hertneck-Dautov, Bad Wiessee 1997. Black only ended up losing this game after overpressing.

**9...♕c8 10 ♗xa8 ♕xa8**

Unlike the Hertneck-Dautov game, White feels that with black's queen bearing down the long diagonal, White's king is safer in the centre of the board.

**11 ♖g1 ♗c8!?**

Why not to more natural b7-square? Well, Black want to move the f6-knight and expel White's knight from e5. For this to work then the d7-pawn needs to be protected.

**12 b3 ♘e4 13 ♗b2 ♘xd2 14 ♔xd2**

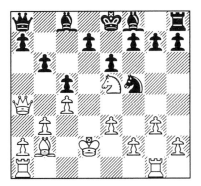

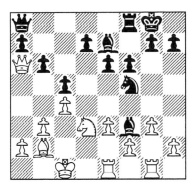

**14...f6**

This was actually the first new move of the game. Timman-Dautov, Forchheim 2000 continued 14...♗e7 15 ♖ad1 f6 16 ♘d3 ♗b7 17 ♔c1 ♗c6 18 ♕a6 0-0 19 h4 ♖b8 20 h5 b5 and Black's dominance along the long diagonal and play on the queenside compensate for the material disadvantage. It's noticeable that Dautov, a strong grandmaster, has been willing to play this position more than once for Black, so he must believe in it.

**15 ♘d3 ♗b7 16 ♖ad1 ♗c6 17 ♕a6 ♗f3**

The light-squared bishop dictates the play along the long diagonal. The reason for Black's last move is that he sees the e1-square as a more passive placing for the white rook. White has a material plus, but it's difficult to organise a suitable plan to make progress.

**18 ♖de1 ♗e7 19 ♔c1 0-0**

In his notes to the game, the Israel IM Alik Gershon points out that, as well as his light square weakness, White's biggest problem is his out of place queen on a6. It's very difficult for White to reintroduce her back into the game.

**20 ♘f4?**

Gershon criticised this move, preferring 20 ♕a3, I guess with the intention of playing ♗c3 and moving the queen back to a reasonable position on b2.

**20...♘d6!**

This knight is heading for the e4-square, where it will attack the f2-pawn.

**21 g4 ♘e4 22 ♘d3 ♗d6**

Note how easy it is to find natural moves for Black. Now the intention is to win back the exchange by capturing on h2.

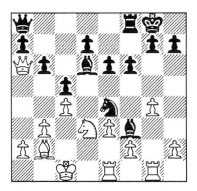

**23 h4**

White sees no way out, so at least he saves the pawn.

**23...♗h2 24 ♖gf1 ♗g2 25 f4**

Or 25 f3 ♗xf1 26 ♖xf1 ♘g3 27 ♖f2

(27 ♖e1 ♕xf3) 27...♗g1 28 ♖g2 ♕xf3 and Black wins – Gershon.

**25...♗g3 26 ♖g1 ♘f2!**

Aseev seems to be toying with Tregubov here. Black has various ways of winning back the exchange; this particular method also trades a pair of knights.

**27 ♘xf2 ♗xf2**

Now the position has clarified. Black wins back the exchange and remains a pawn up. Certainly Black's decision to sacrifice in the early part of the game has paid off handsomely.

**28 ♗c3**

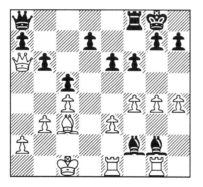

**28...♕b7?!**

This move seems a little inconsistent with what has gone on before. With White's queen so poorly placed and his king out in the open, it looks a little strange to offer a queen exchange to reach an opposite coloured bishops ending. Black's advantage remains substantial, but I prefer Gershon's recommendation of 28...♗xe1 29 ♖xe1 ♕e4!, and if 30 ♕xa7 then 30...♕d3 31 ♔b2 ♗e4! completes Black's domination of the light squares very nicely.

**29 ♕xb7 ♗xb7 30 g5 ♗xe1 31 ♖xe1 fxg5 32 hxg5 ♗e4**

Black's light square dominance continues into the endgame. The bishop is very well placed on e4, pointing at all four corners of the board.

**33 ♗e5 d5 34 ♖d1 ♖d8 35 ♔b2 ♔f7**

Black's eventual plan will be to march his king unopposed on the light squares deep into enemy territory with ...♔g6-f5-g4-f3.

**36 ♔c3 ♖d7 37 a3 a5 38 b4**

It's understandable that White wishes to trade as many pawns as possible, but now Black is able to open another avenue of attack. White was better off sitting tight and waiting.

**38...axb4+ 39 axb4 ♖a7!**

Taking the open file.

**40 bxc5 bxc5 41 ♔b3 ♔g6**

White has a long hard struggle to defend this position a pawn down. White's next move ensures this is not necessary as he blunders a piece.

**42 ♗d6?? ♖d7 0-1**

Bishop moves are met by 43...dxc4+ and ...♖xd1.

### Bishops of Opposite Colour

Most chessplayers know that bishops of opposite colour often produce endgames with drawish tendencies, especially pure bishop endings. On occasions a player can be up to three pawns ahead and can still only manage to draw.

Here's a rather contrived position to make the point.

Despite being three pawns to the good, White can make no progress in this position. The only way forward is with 1 f6, but then 1...♗xf6! 2 ♔xf6 results in stalemate.

Less common is the knowledge that the presence of opposite coloured bishops in a middlegame can have anything but a drawish effect. When one player is attacking, especially on the same colour of square as his bishop, it can often seem as if the attacker has an extra piece. Here is such an example.

**Gligoric-Honfi**
The Hague 1966

Despite Black apparent activity in the diagram position, it is White who has a clear advantage. The problem for Black is that his king has less cover than White's. White's attack will not be immediate, but when it comes Black will have all sorts of long term problems trying to defend on the dark squares. The presence of opposite coloured bishops will virtually give White an extra piece when he attacks Black vulnerable dark squares on the kingside.

**20 ♗c3**

A good start, putting the bishop on the long diagonal.

**20...♖e2**

This looks impressive but Black's activity is short-lived.

**21 ♕h6 ♕f8 22 ♕h4!**

Naturally White declines to exchange queens as Black weak king will suffer much more in the middlegame than in the ending.

**22...♕c5+ 23 ♔h1 ♖f8**

Preventing ♕f6.

**24 ♖ad1 ♗d5 25 ♕h6 ♖f7 26 ♖fe1!**

Now White gradually assumes the initiative.

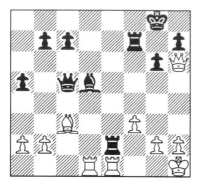

**26...♖xe1+ 27 ♖xe1**

Now Black must deal with the threat of ♖e8+.

**27...♖e7 28 ♖d1**

Again White is loath to exchange pieces and thus ease Black's defensive burden. Now the bishop on d5 dare not move as this would allow ♖d8+.

**28...c6 29 ♕f4 ♖e6**

Once again Black must prevent infiltration on the dark squares with ♕f6.

**30 h3 ♕f8 31 ♕d4 ♕h6**

**32 a4**

White fixes the pawn on a5 and moves his own pawn from attack on a2. It's noticeable that White does not have to worry about the speed of his attack. Black's dark square weaknesses on the

kingside will not go away and, as long as White avoids exchanges, he will keep a long term attack against the black king.

**32...g5**

Strangely enough, Black's only chance of counterplay lies with exposing his king further by moving pawns on the kingside. To make any dent in the white camp Black needs to play ...g6-g5, ...h7-h5 and then ....g5-g4. It doesn't take a genius to work out that this plan isn't likely to succeed.

**33 ♗xa5 ♕g7 34 ♕f2**

Again, despite now being a pawn up, it pays White to keep the queens on. Black would have far more drawing chances in an endgame.

**34...h5 35 ♗c3 ♕g6 36 ♔g1 ♕f5**

The immediate 36...g4 loses after 37 fxg4 hxg4 38 ♖f1 ♖e8 39 ♕h4, when there is no good defence to mate with ♕h8.

**37 ♕d4 ♕g6 38 a5 ♖e8**

Or 38...g4 39 fxg4 hxg4 40 ♕h8+ ♔f7 41 ♖f1+ ♔e7 42 ♕f8+ ♔d7 43 ♖f7+ and White wins.

**39 b4 ♔h7**

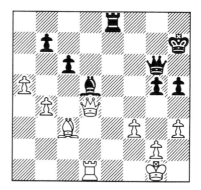

**40 b5!**

Attacking on a second front is immediately decisive. White aims to create a passed pawn on the queenside.

**40...♔g8 41 a6! bxa6 42 bxa6 g4**

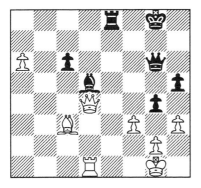

Finally this lunge arrives, but it is too late.

**43 fxg4 ♖e2**

43...hxg4 44 ♖f1 ♔h7 45 hxg4 prevents any counterplay – the a6-pawn will be decisive.

**44 ♕h8+ ♔f7 45 ♖f1+ ♔e7 46 ♗f6+ 1-0**

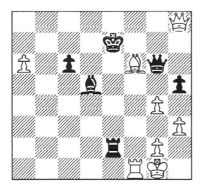

White wins after either 46...♔d6 47 ♕f8+ ♔d7 48 ♕d8+ ♔e6 49 ♕e7 mate, or 46...♔e6 47 ♕c8+ ♔f7 48 ♗d4+ ♔e7 49 ♗c5+.

**Prophylaxis**

I've noticed that I've used this term quite a few times throughout the book, so perhaps it's time for an explanation. It was Nimzowitsch who used this word to describe a certain strategic idea: 'the anticipation, prevention or determent of the opponent's threats' – *The Oxford Companion to Chess*.

In virtually every game prophylactic measures are taken. Take, for example, the opening moves of the Ruy Lopez, one of the most famous openings of all time.

**1 e4 e5 2 ♘f3 ♘c6 3 ♗b5 a6 4 ♗a4 ♘f6 5 0-0 ♗e7 6 ♖e1**

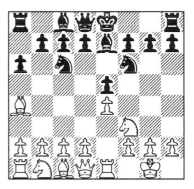

Of course the main reason behind White's rook move is to protect the attacked e4-pawn. But 6 ♖e1 is also a prophylactic measure, dissuading Black from contemplating the freeing advance ...d7-d5, as after exd5 White's rook will directly pressurise Black's e-pawn.

Some grandmasters' styles are heavily based on prophylaxis. World Champion Tigran Petrosian was a wizard at frustrating his opponents by preventing their active ideas. Anatoly Karpov is also very good at 'doing nothing', as it's sometimes called by those who don't understand his play.

Let's take a look at a couple of more complex examples of prophylaxis. The main line of Larsen Variation in the Philidor Defence goes as follows:

**1 e4 e5 2 ♘f3 d6 3 d4 exd4 4 ♘xd4 g6 5 ♘c3 ♗g7 6 ♗e3 ♘f6 7 ♕d2 0-0 8 0-0-0 ♘c6 9 f3 ♘xd4 10 ♗xd4 ♗e6**

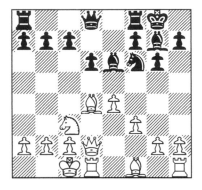

This position, which has many similarities to the main line Dragon Sicilian, has produced excellent results for White, but I can't help feeling that Black's chances have been underestimated in this line.

Theoretically speaking 11 g4 has been the normal move for White here. After the active 11...c5! 12 ♗e3 ♕a5 the game becomes very complex and in *Winning with the Philidor* Tony Kosten makes a good case for Black's position. This ultra sharp stuff may still be good for White, but it also may not be everyone's cup of tea.

In the game Chernin-Zaitshik, Lvov 1987, White came up with the prophylactic move 11 ♗e3!. Basically, this move takes measures against the ...c7-c5 thrust *before* Black actually plays the move, and thus Black's counterplay on the queenside has been nullified very efficiently. 11...c5? 12 ♕xd6 ♕a5 13 ♕xc5 just leaves Black two pawns down for no

compensation, while Zaitshik's 11...♖e8 12 ♗g5! ♕e7 13 g4 also left White with a clear advantage.

Kasparov is known as a very dynamic player, but it was he who produced one of the most amazing pieces of prophylaxis in a crucial world championship clash with Karpov.

**Karpov-Kasparov**
Moscow (24th matchgame) 1985

Karpov required a win in this final encounter in order to retain his world title, so stakes were exceedingly high. Keeping his cool under extreme pressure, Kasparov now produced a magnificent prophylactic measure. Rooks belong on open files, right? Then what can we make of the game continuation?
**23...♖e7!! 24 ♔g1 ♖ce8!!**

What on earth are black's two rooks doing huddled behind the e6-pawn? We realise the answer when we look at White's attack. The only real method for White to continue the attack is with f4-f5. Kasparov's last two moves simply prevent White from carrying out this idea. Without this option, Karpov's attack stutters and Kasparov eventually wins a historic game.

**25 ℤd1**

25 f5? exf5 26 exf5 ♗xg2 27 ♔xg2 ♗xc3 28 bxc3 ♘d5 wins for Black, as moving the bishop allows ...ℤe2.

**25...f5 26 gxf6 ♘xf6 27 ℤg3 ℤf7 28 ♗xb6 ♛b8 29 ♗e3 ♘h5 30 ℤg4 ♘f6 31 ℤh4 g5 32 fxg5 ♘g4 33 ♛d2 ♘xe3 34 ♛xe3 ♘xc2 35 ♛b6 ♗a8 36 ℤxd6 ℤb7 37 ♛xa6 ℤxb3 38 ℤxe6**

**38...ℤxb2 39 ♛c4 ♔h8 40 e5 ♛a7+ 41 ♔h1 ♗xg2+ 42 ♔xg2 ♘d4+ 0-1**

## Positional Sacrifices

This is another subject about which at least one whole book has been written. I'll just content myself with a few examples. Positional sacrifices, as opposed to tactical ones, usually produce long term structural compensation rather than immediate attacks on the king, although there are occasions when both are produced. Examples of positional sacrifices include pawn sacrifices in order to gain outposts or even to prevent an opponent claiming an outpost (see the first two examples). Another common theme is an exchange sacrifice in order to inflict pawn weaknesses on an unfortunate opponent.

**A.Hoffman-Rodi**
Mar del Plata 2001

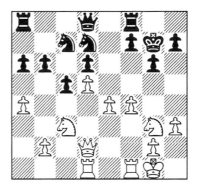

Both sides have pawn majorities: Black's is on the queenside, White's is in the centre. Black is ready to play ...b7-b5. How should White proceed in the centre? 20 ℤde1 suggests itself, planning the advance e4-e5. 20 f5 also looks an aggressive way of continuing, but this does allow Black to plonk a very useful defensive knight on e5. 20...♘e5 21 f6+ ♔h8 22 ♛h6 ℤg8 23 ℤf4 ♛f8 is not that convincing. Is there another way?

**20 e5!**

This type of pawn sacrifice is now very typical in positions with this pawn structure.

**20...dxe5 21 f5!**

For the pawn deficit White has four major pluses:

1) He has a powerful passed d-pawn

2) The e4-square can be used as a very useful outpost for the white knights

3) Compared to lines with 20 f5, Black has no defensive outpost of his own

4) White has an automatic and slow burning attack against the black king.

**21...♘e8 22 ♘ce4 f6 23 h4!**

White plans to soften up the black kingside with h4-h5.

**23...b5**

Finally Black begins operations on the queenside, but these are woefully inadequate. The real action is on the other side.

**24 axb5 axb5 25 fxg6 hxg6 26 h5!**

Now the f5-square will become White's property as well.

**26...g5**

After 26...f5 27 ♘g5 ♘c7 28 d6 Black can resign.

**27 ♘f5+ ♔h7 28 ♕c2**

The position of white's knights is really a sight for sore eyes. Despite being a pawn to the good, Black is positionally bust here. White's last move lines up some nasty discovered attacks along the b1-h7 diagonal.

**20...c4**

Missing White's idea. 28...♔h8 is more resilient, although 29 ♘xc5 ♕b6 30 b4 leaves White in complete command.

**29 ♘xg5+! ♔h8**

Or 29...fxg5 30 ♘h6+! ♔h8 (30...♔xh6 allows mate with 31 ♕g6) 31 ♖xf8+ ♘xf8 32 ♘f7+ and White wins the queen.

**30 ♘e6 ♕b6+ 31 ♔h1**

White's knights are absolute monsters. The rest of the game is quite gruesome for Black.

**31...♖f7 32 ♘h6 ♖h7 33 ♕g6**

Threatening ♕g8 mate.

**33...♘g7**

**34 ♖xf6! ♘xf6 35 ♕xf6 ♕e3**

35...b4 36 ♖f1 ♕b8 37 ♘f8 ♕e8 38 ♘g6+ ♕xg6 39 ♕f8+ ♖xf8 40 ♖xf8 mate is a nice finish, although of course White has other more ordinary ways to win.

**36 ♘g5 1-0**

**Halkias-Erdogan**
Antalya 2001

A similar situation to the previous example. How does White exploit his pawn majority in the centre?

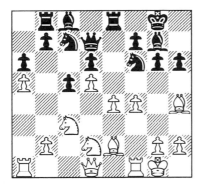

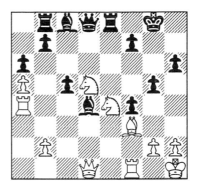

**16 ♗xf6!**

It seems strange to give up the dark-squared bishop for a knight, but this is just the start of a forcing sequence which allows White to make the crucial break-through.

**16...♗xf6 17 e5!**

On first sight this advance looks impossible, but the positional considerations dictate that that the tactics work for White.

**17...♗g7**

17...dxe5 18 ♘de4 ♗g7 transposes.

**18 ♘de4 dxe5**

There is no other option as White was threatening to capture on d6.

**19 d6 exf4**

Black gives up a piece, but alternatives aren't convincing, for example 19...♘e6 20 ♘d5 (threatening ♘f6+) 20...♕d8 21 fxe5 and White renews the threat of ♘f6+.

**20 dxc7 ♗d4+ 21 ♔h1 ♕xc7**

Black has three pawns for the piece, but he has no good pawn majority and White is very much in control.

**22 ♘d5 ♕d8 23 ♗f3 g5 24 ♖a4**

White simply wants to capture on d4 when Black will be fatally exposed on the dark squares.

**24...♗g7**

24...♗xb2 25 ♕e2 ♗d4 26 ♘ef6+ wins more material.

**25 ♘xc5 ♖e5 26 ♖d4 g4 27 ♗e4 ♖h5 28 ♖xf4 f5 29 ♗c2**

Now White is easily winning and the rest of the game is of little importance.

**29...♕xa5 30 ♘e7+ ♔h8 31 b4 ♕a3 32 ♖xg4! ♕e3**

32...fxg4 33 ♖d8+ ♗f8 34 ♕d1 mates.

**33 ♖d8+ ♔h7 34 ♖xc8 ♖xc8 35 ♗xf5+ ♔h8 36 ♗xc8 ♕xe7 37 ♖e4 ♕f8 38 ♕e2 ♕d6 39 ♕xh5 1-0**

**Chernin-Hertneck**
Austrian League 2000

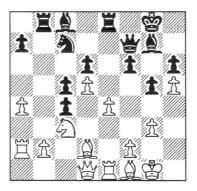

Black looks to be in a bad way here.

His kingside is full of weaknesses, his bishop on g7 is blocked in and White has just moved his bishop from g2 to f1, attacking the weak c4-pawn. How should Black react?

**26...f5!?**

Black's best chance, and much stronger than simply defending the c4-pawn with 26...♗a6. With 26...f5 Black sacrifices an irrelevant pawn and in return strives for a powerful bind on the kingside.

**27 ♗xc4 f4!**

Another excellent move. Now the bishop on g7 can settle on the e5-outpost.

**28 ♕f3 ♗e5 29 g4?**

I really don't like this move, after which Black can simply build up his position at leisure. White must try to fight back on the kingside with 29 gxf4 gxf4 30 ♔h1 ♔h7 31 ♖g1.

**29...♖e7**

Only Black has winning chances now.

**30 ♗e2 ♘e8 31 ♕g2 ♘f6 32 ♘b5?**

Despite leaving some dark square weaknesses around the white king, 32 f3 just had to be played.

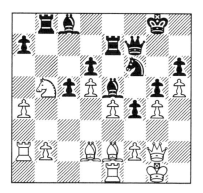

**32...a6!**

Naturally!

**33 ♘a3**

33 ♘c3 ♗xc3 34 ♗xc3 ♘xe4 35 ♗f3 ♘xc3 36 ♖xe7 ♕xe7 37 bxc3 ♕e1+ is also very good for Black.

**33...♖xb2 34 ♗c4 ♖xa2 35 ♗xa2 ♘xg4**

Now White's pawns start to drop off like ripe apples...it's game over.

**36 ♘c4 ♕xh5 37 ♕h1 ♕xh1+ 38 ♔xh1 ♘xf2+ 39 ♔g2 ♘d3 40 ♖b1 ♖b7 41 ♖xb7 ♗xb7 42 ♗b1 ♘b4 43 ♘xe5 dxe5 44 ♗c3 ♘xd5!**

The simplest. Black's pawns are way too strong.

**45 exd5 ♗xd5+ 46 ♔f2 e4 47 ♗c2 ♔f7 48 a5 ♔e6 49 ♗a4**

**49...g4 0-1**

50 ♗e8 e3+ 51 ♔g1 f3 wins easily.

In this final example we see Garry Kasparov implementing a typical exchange sacrifice for long-term structural advantages.

**Movsesian-Kasparov**
Sarajevo 2000
*Sicilian Defence*

1 e4 c5 2 ♘f3 d6 3 d4 cxd4 4 ♘xd4 ♘f6 5 ♘c3 a6 6 ♗e3 e6 7 f3 b5 8

♕d2 ♞bd7 9 0-0-0 ♝b7 10 g4 ♞b6
11 ♕f2 ♞fd7 12 ♔b1 ♜c8 13 ♝d3

### 13...♜xc3!?

A typical sacrifice, for which the Sicilian Defence must hold a patent. In fact this sacrifice is seen more often in the Dragon Variation (1 e4 c5 2 ♞f3 d6 3 d4 cxd4 4 ♞xd4 ♞f6 5 ♞c3 g6), but it can be just as effective in lines such as Kasparov's choice of the Najdorf.

I guess I would say that the sacrifice is both positional and tactical. Of course Black will have good tactical chances against White's weakened king, but the crippling of the white pawns on the queenside is certainly positional in nature.

### 14 bxc3 ♕c7 15 ♞e2 ♝e7 16 g5 0-0 17 h4

Such is the state of opening theory these days that only Kasparov's next move takes the game into unknown territory.

### 17...♞a4!

This move improves upon 17...d5 18 h5 dxe4 19 ♝xe4 ♝xe4 20 fxe4 ♞c4 21 ♝c1 b4 22 cxb4 ♝xb4 23 ♜h3, which was good for White in Zagrebelny-Lingnau, Berlin 1993.

### 18 ♝c1?!

This defensive measure was criticised by Ftacnik, who prefers 18 h5 ♞e5 19 h6 g6, when the assessment of 'unclear' has never been more appropriate.

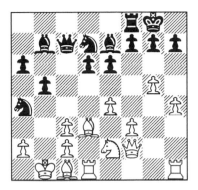

### 18...♞e5 19 h5 d5!

Kasparov hits out in the centre just as Movsesian was starting to threaten on the kingside.

### 20 ♕h2

If 20 h6 Black naturally blocks White's attack with 20...g6.

### 20...♝d6 21 ♕h3 ♞xd3 22 cxd3

22 ♜xd3? dxe4, unleashing the bishop on b7, is very strong for Black.

### 22...b4!

Kasparov opens up the queenside even more. This is stronger than the more obvious 22...♞xc3+, with Ftacnik giving the variation 23 ♞xc3 ♕xc3 24 ♝b2 ♕b4 25 g6 ♝e5 (25...dxc4? 26 h6! ♝e5 27 d4 is a winning attack for White – such is the fine line between success and failure) 26 d4 ♝f4 27 gxf7+ ♔xf7 28 ♕g4 ♝h6, again with an unclear assessment.

### 23 cxb4 ♜c8 24 ♔a1 dxe4

24...♝xb4!? also looks strong, for example 25 ♕h2 ♕c2 (threatening ...♞c3) 26 ♜de1 ♝xe1 27 ♜xe1 ♕xd3 and Black must be winning.

**25 fxe4**

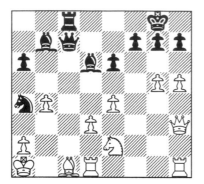

**25...♗xe4!**

A thunderbolt. Of course the bishop cannot be captured.

**26 g6**

A desperate attempt at counterplay. Other moves lose quickly:

a) 26 dxe4 ♗e5+ 27 ♔b1 ♕c2 mate.

b) 26 ♖hg1 ♕c2 27 ♘d4 ♗e5 28 dxe4 ♗xd4+ 29 ♖xd4 ♕xc1+ 30 ♖xc1 ♖xc1 mate.

**26...♗xh1 27 ♕xh1 ♗xb4 28 gxf7+ ♔f8**

28...♕xf7 is also good enough, but Kasparov uses the white pawn on f7 as a shield for his own king.

**29 ♕g2 ♖b8!**

Material is now level, but White's king is still far more exposed. Kasparov makes no mistakes and finishes off the game cleanly.

**30 ♗b2 ♘xb2 31 ♘d4**

Or 31 ♔xb2 ♗d2+ 32 ♔a1 ♗c3+ and Black wins.

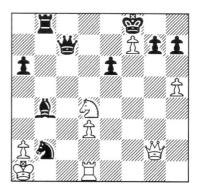

**31...♘xd1!**

Typically, Kasparov finishes off with another combination.

**32 ♘xe6+ ♔xf7 0-1**

Black wins after 33 ♕xg7+ ♔xe6 34 ♕xc7 ♗c3+, or 33 ♘xc7 ♗c3+.